JUDEO-SPANISH BALLADS FROM NEW YORK

JUDEO-SPANISH BALLADS
FROM NEW YORK

Collected by

Maír José Benardete

Edited, with Introduction and Notes, by

SAMUEL G. ARMISTEAD   and   JOSEPH H. SILVERMAN

UNIVERSITY OF CALIFORNIA PRESS
BERKELEY   LOS ANGELES   LONDON

The publication of this volume was supported
in part by a grant from the
Memorial Foundation for Jewish Culture.

University of California Press
Berkeley and Los Angeles, California

University of California Press, Ltd.
London, England

Library of Congress Cataloging in Publication Data
Main entry under title:

Judeo-Spanish ballads from New York.

  Includes ballads in Ladino with romanized text.
  Bibliography: p. 119
  Includes indexes.
  1. Ballads, Ladino—New York (City)   I. Benardete,
Maír José, 1895—   .   II Armistead, Samuel G., 1927—
III. Silverman, Joseph H., 1924—
PC4813.7.J8   861'.044'08   80-28714
ISBN 0-520-04348-0

Printed in the United States of America

1   2   3   4   5   6   7   8   9

CONTENTS

PREFACE

The Sephardic community of New York City is, without doubt, an excellent source of balladic material, given that there are representative numbers of families from all the Eastern Judeo-Spanish settlements, as well as from Morocco.[1] As a matter of fact, there exist throughout the city beneficent societies for groups from such locations as Salonika, Monastir, Istanbul, Adrianopolis, Silivri, Gallipoli, Dardanelles, Ankara, Smyrna, Chios, Rhodes, and so on. These places would scarcely tempt any scholar, since the cost of a research trip to collect ballads in such remote sites would surely be prohibitive. But unstable political conditions in the Eastern Mediterranean area during the early years of this century gave impetus to the emigration of Jews from Turkey and the Balkan countries to the United States and to South America. So it is convenient that in New York City, with a Sephardic population of approximately twenty-five thousand, only time and patience are needed to interview native informants from all these distant communities.[2]

And yet this bright view must be qualified by several factors: a large number of young male Sephardic immigrants who do not sing ballads, the negative linguistic influence of the French-oriented Alliance Israélite Universelle, and

---

[1]The Preface adapts certain passages from the original introduction to Professor Benardete's thesis. Thus it reflects, at various points, the circumstances of the early 1920s.

[2]In a report prepared under the auspices of the Bureau of Jewish Social Research on behalf of the New York Federation, Louis M. Hacker stated that there were, according to conservative estimates, approximately forty thousand Sephardic Jews in New York City at the time of his investigation. Dr. Hacker indicated, on the basis of rather sketchy immigration figures, that between 1899 and 1925, 25,591 men, women, and children of Sephardic origin entered the United States from Turkey, Bulgaria, Serbia, Montenegro, and Greece. See "The Communal Life of the Sephardic Jews in New York City," *Journal of Jewish Communal Service*, 3 (1926), 32–40: 32 and 34. For more details on this period, see Joseph M. Papo, "The Sephardic Jewish Community of New York," *Studies in Sephardic Culture: The David N. Barocas Memorial Volume*, edited by Marc D. Angel (New York: Sepher-Hermon Press, 1980), pp. 65–94. [Note of SGA and JHS.]

the deleterious effects of the phonograph on folk traditions. As one elderly woman who sang for me explained, many ballads have disappeared because "los fonógrafos nos siegaron los garones" ("phonographs have cut our throats," i.e., for singing). In truth, the phonograph has done away with the need to learn ballads by heart and, because of its easy availability and reasonable price, it has become the new source of family entertainment. Although the fondness for *romances* continues among the Sephardim of New York, the phonograph record—as performed by singers who scarcely know the lyrics and are accompanied by Turkish instruments, playing Turkish melodies—now prevails over the traditional family singer. So a heavy influx of young immigrants, a dearth of elderly singers, a growing interest in French and, of course, English, and the attractiveness of readily available phonograph records have all led inexorably to a marked decline in traditional ballad singing.

The Sephardic Jews of New York live in each of the city's boroughs, particularly in Manhattan, Brooklyn, and the Bronx, as well as in its numerous outlying districts. It is not easy to locate them and most have a distinctively Hispano-Arabic sense of the sanctity of the home, zealously guarding their privacy. For these reasons, it has taken considerable effort to make contact with ballad singers.

In general, I collected my ballads from women, most of them of at least forty years of age and some with excellent repertoires. Mrs. Moché, from Salonika, whom I visited three times, gave the most texts—twenty-two altogether—even inviting me back to her home once again because she had remembered three more *romansas*. A young married lady, Mrs. Moreno, from Izmir, gave me seven texts; Mrs. Rica Levy, from Tangier, eight; Mrs. Fihma, from Tetuán, seven. Mrs. Rosina Sedacca and Mrs. Levy, from Dardanelles (Çanakkale) offered me their variants, as did Mrs. Aboulafia, from Gallipoli.

Now, after almost sixty years, it is a source of great satisfaction that this collection should become available to ballad scholars in published form.

Maír José Benardete

INTRODUCTION

It hardly seems necessary to insist on the crucial importance of the Judeo-Spanish ballad tradition to the study of both Pan-Hispanic and Pan-European balladry. The present-day Spanish-speaking Sephardim of Morocco, the Balkans, and the Near East are the descendants of Jews exiled from Spain at the end of the Middle Ages (in 1492). Their archaic, highly conservative ballad repertoires preserve many features of the Spanish ballad tradition as it existed at the time of their exile from the Iberian Peninsula. Numerous narrative types dating back to medieval times have thus survived among the Sephardic Jews, while they have, in many cases, disappeared from all other branches of the Hispanic ballad tradition. A thorough exploration of the Judeo-Spanish ballad corpus is, then, essential to the task of filling the rather substantial gaps that still exist in our knowledge of late medieval and sixteenth-century Spanish balladry. The Sephardic tradition is also, of course, crucially important to comparative studies of the various other modern branches of Pan-Hispanic balladry: the Spanish, Hispano-American, Portuguese, and Catalan traditions. At the same time, Judeo-Spanish narrative poetry, of all the various Hispanic sub-traditions, is also one of the most significant for comparative Pan-European ballad studies. Because of its conservatism, Sephardic balladry preserves a number of thematic correspondences to other European ballad traditions which are no longer in evidence in most other geographic branches of the Hispanic *Romancero*. Judeo-Spanish balladry can, then, frequently provide clues to thematic relationships on a Pan-European, as well as on a Pan-Hispanic, scale.[1]

Besides its important conservatism, as an archaic lateral tradition, another previously neglected aspect of the Judeo-Spanish ballad should also be taken into account. This is its eclectic character, its absorption of narrative themes and stylistic features borrowed from the popular poetry of the peoples among whom the Sephardim lived after their exile from Spain: namely from Greek,

---

[1] See Samuel G. Armistead, "The Importance of Hispanic Balladry to International Ballad Research," *3. Arbeitstagung über Fragen des Typenindex der europäischen Volksballaden*, ed. Rolf W. Brednich et al. (Berlin: Staatliches Institut für Musikforschung, 1970), pp. 48–52; Idem, "Judeo-Spanish and Pan-European Balladry," *JVF*, 24 (1979), 127–138; and a number of chapters in our *The Judeo-Spanish Ballad Chapbooks of Yacob Abraham Yoná* (Berkeley, Los Angeles, London: University of California Press, 1971).

3

Turkish, and Arabic.[2] Although the survival of medieval text-types constitutes one of the important facets of the Sephardic tradition, it should not impede the recognition of other characteristics of Judeo-Spanish balladry. In a fundamental review of recent scholarship, Diego Catalán has pointed out important innovative features coexisting with archaic elements, particularly in Eastern Mediterranean Sephardic balladry.[3] With the publication of Paul Bénichou's pathfinding *Creación poética en el romancero tradicional* (Madrid: Gredos, 1968)—based in many cases on Judeo-Spanish evidence—the Sephardic *romancero* emerges also as essential to the study of creativity in Hispanic traditional poetry.[4]

Of all the widely separated areas of the twentieth-century Sephardic diaspora, none has been more explored and none has yielded a greater harvest of Judeo-Spanish folk-poetry than the United States. Israel,[5] Spain,[6] France,[7]

---

[2]On this problem, see especially S. G. Armistead and J. H. Silverman, "Exclamaciones turcas y otros rasgos orientales en el romancero judeoespañol," *Sef*, 30 (1970), 177–193.

[3]"Memoria e invención en el Romancero de tradición oral," *RPh*, 24 (1970–71), 1–25, 441–463.

[4]See, for example, the studies by Diego Catalán, Suzanne Petersen, Antonio Sánchez Romeralo, Braulio do Nascimento, Giuseppe Di Stefano, and Paul Bénichou in *El Romancero en la tradición oral moderna: Ier Coloquio internacional*, ed. D. Catalán, S. G. Armistead, and A. Sánchez Romeralo (Madrid: C.S.M.P., 1973), pp. 151–301.

[5]For Israel, the largest collection is that of Israel J. Katz, formed in 1959–1961 and 1971: some 250 texts collected from both Eastern and Moroccan informants. Of this collection, some 80 texts are not "diasporic," but are from Sabra informants, native to the Old City of Jerusalem. The rest of the collection consists of some 50 texts from Moroccan informants resident in Israel; and 120 from Eastern immigrants. In the summer of 1978, we collected some 205 texts during two weeks of intensive fieldwork (19 Sabra, 89 Eastern, and 97 Moroccan texts). See our publications, "Field Notes on a Ballad Expedition to Israel," *Shevet va'Am*, 4(9) (1980), and "The Judeo-Spanish *Romancero* in Israel," *La Corónica*, 7:2 (Spring 1979), 105–106; reproduced in *Echoes* (Jerusalem), no. 9 (October 1979), 12–14. Most, if not all, of Isaac Levy's published collection (93 *romances*) was formed in Israel (*Chants judéo-espagnols*, 4 vols., London: Fédération Séphardite Mondiale, 1959, and Jerusalem: Édition de l'auteur, 1970–1973). Five of Levy's published texts are identified as being from Jerusalem (i.e., Sabra versions); 8 are from the Moroccan tradition. (Note our reviews: *NRFH*, 14 [1960], 345–349; *Sef*, 31 [1971], 462–464; *ESef*, 1 [1978], 247–248.) We do not know the extent of his unedited ballad recordings. Moshe Attias's fine *Romancero sefaradí: Romances y cantes populares en judeo-español* (Jerusalem: Instituto Ben-Zewi, 1956; 2d ed., 1961)—76 *romance* texts—is based on versions provided by four informants (two from Salónica and two from Larissa) resident in Israel (see p. 331). Oro A. Librowicz collected 14 Moroccan ballads at Migdal Ha-Emek (Israel). Florette M. Rechnitz has also collected Moroccan ballads in Israel ("Tres romances de Tánger," *ESef*, 1 [1978], 121–128; with musicological transcriptions and commentary by Israel J. Katz, pp. 129–131) and Reginetta Haboucha has formed a collection of 35 Eastern texts (12 of which are from Sabra informants), representing 13 text-types ("Judeo-Spanish Ballads from Israel," *El Romancero hoy: Nuevas fronteras*, ed. Antonio Sánchez Romeralo, S. G. Armistead, and Diego Catalán, Madrid: C.S.M.P., 1979). As of now we know of some 676 ballad texts collected in Israel (338 from Eastern immigrants; 116 Sabra texts; 172 from Moroccan immigrants).

Batya Maoz is also collecting *romances* from Eastern informants in Israel; see *Šîrê 'am sĕfārādiyîm šel yĕhûdê 'arçôt ha-Balkan*, M.A. thesis, Hebrew University, Jerusalem, 1976. For

England,[8] Holland,[9] Belgium,[10] Canada,[11] Cuba,[12] Mexico,[13] Venezuela,[14] Uruguay,[15] Argentina, Paraguay,[16] Rhodesia, and South Africa,[17] all have Sephardic immigrant communities of relatively recent origin, but none has been explored in such depth or by so many ballad fieldworkers as those of the

---

more on the ballad tradition of Israel, see our article, "Judeo-Spanish Ballads in a MS. by Salomon Israel Cherezli," *Studies in Honor of M. J. Benardete*, ed. Izaak A. Langnas and Barton Sholod (New York: Las Américas, 1965), pp. 367—387 (edited now, with extensive additional commentary, in *Tres calas en el romancero sefardí (Rodas, Jerusalén, Estados Unidos)*, Madrid: Castalia, 1979).

[6]A substantial portion (64 texts) of Oro Anahory Librowicz's Moroccan collection was recorded in Málaga and Marbella. She has also done some recording in Madrid (36 texts). See her "Florilegio de romances sefardíes de la diáspora" (Ph.D. diss., Columbia University, 1974); revised as *Florilegio de romances sefardíes de la diáspora (Una colección malagueña)* (Madrid: C.S.M.P., 1980). Before undertaking our Moroccan fieldwork in 1962, we collected a few ballads from Tetuán informants in Madrid. More work doubtless remains to be done in the Madrid community; productive collecting could also be carried out in Barcelona and perhaps in Seville. On Sephardic communities in Spain, see Haim Vidal Sephiha's excellent book, *L'Agonie des judéo-espagnols* (Paris: Editions Entente, 1977), pp. 86—87.

[7]Cf. Martine Cohen, *Recueil, edition et étude de textes enregistrés auprés de judéo-hispano-phones originaires de Turquie et de Grèce à Paris en 1972*, "Mémoire," Université de Paris IV: Institut d'Etudes Hispaniques, Paris, 1972—1973, which includes four ballad texts representing five text-types. A systematic ballad survey of French communities would probably yield interesting results. Cf. Sephiha, *L'Agonie*, pp. 88—92. For a recent report, see Miriam Zehavi, "North African Jews in France and Israel," *Challenge* (Jerusalem), 3:9 (July 1979), 4—5.

[8]Except for an interesting, still unedited interview of a Salonikan informant conducted for us by Margaret Chaplin, there has been no collecting of Judeo-Spanish ballads in England to our knowledge. On the diverse Sephardic communities of London, see Issachar Ben-Ami, "Death, Burial and Mourning Customs among Sephardic Jews in London," *Studies in the Cultural Life of the Jews in England: Folklore Research Center Studies*, 5 (Jerusalem, 1975), 11—36; also Albert Hyamson, *The Sephardim of England* (London: Methuen, 1951), pp. 403—415; Sephiha, *L'Agonie*, pp. 85—86.

[9]There is apparently a small community of recent immigrants in Holland. See Chanah Milner and Paul Storm, *Sefardische liederen en balladen (Romanzas)* (The Hague: Albersen, 1974), p. 114. Concerning this collection, note our critical review (with Israel J. Katz) in *Musica Judaica* (New York), 2:1 (1977—78), 95—99. All of the texts included in Milner—Storm are secondhand and none was recorded in Holland. On remnants of an early (seventeenth-century) Hispano-Judaic ballad tradition in Amsterdam, see our article, "El Romancero entre los sefardíes de Holanda," *Etudes . . . offertes à Jules Horrent* (Liège, 1980), pp. 535—541. For an overview of Sephardic Jewry in Amsterdam, see J. A. Van Praag, *Los sefarditas de Amsterdam y sus actividades* (Madrid: Universidad de Madrid, 1967).

[10]On the Sephardic community in Belgium, see Albert Doppagne, "Le Judéo-espagnol en Belgique," *XI Congreso Internacional de Lingüística y Filología Románicas: Actas*, 4, ed. Antonio Quilis (Madrid: *RFE*, Anejo 86, 1968), 2141—2144; also Sephiha, *L'Agonie*, p. 85. To our knowledge, no ballad fieldwork has been done.

[11]Oro A. Librowicz has collected a few Moroccan *romances* (8 texts) in Montreal, but much work remains to be done, especially in the large Toronto Moroccan community. See Sephiha, *L'Agonie*, p. 94.

[12]There was a large Eastern Sephardic community in Cuba; many of these people have immigrated to the United States and to Spanish America. For interviews with two Turkish informants in Havana, carried out by Roberto Esquenazi Mayo, April 7 and 8, 1937 (which yielded four ballads, embodying six text-types), see S. G. Armistead et al., *El romancero judeo-español en*

United States (and many have not been explored at all). Only the multisecular Sephardic homelands of the Eastern Mediterranean and North Africa have produced larger collections of ballads than those brought together in the United States.[18]

---

el Archivo Menéndez Pidal, 3 vols. (Madrid: C.S.M.P., 1978), III, 147 (subsequently cited as CMP).

[13]No interviews with Sephardic informants in the large Mexico City community have so far yielded ballads. Cf. Sephiha, *L'Agonie*, p. 95.

[14]Oro A. Librowicz has collected 102 Moroccan ballad texts in Caracas. More work could undoubtedly be done there.

[15]Mónica E. Hollander has thoroughly explored the Montevideo community. See her "Reliquias del romancero judeo-español de Oriente" (Ph.D. diss., University of Pennsylvania, 1978). The texts included in Jacobo Politi and Daniel Aljanati, *Selección de romanzas y poesía litúrgica sefarditas* (Montevideo: Comunidad Israelita Sefardí, 1974), are all secondhand, being reproductions from publications of Isaac Levy.

[16]Ismael Moya's rich, but poorly edited, *Romancero: Estudios sobre materiales de la colección de folklore*, 2 vols. (Buenos Aires: Universidad, 1941), includes 5 *romances* provided by Sephardic informants in Buenos Aires (II, 255−259). Most of the texts in Paul Bénichou's splendid *Romancero judeo-español de Marruecos* (Madrid: Castalia, 1968), originally collected in the early 1940s, were provided by Moroccan informants in Buenos Aires (see p. 14). Recently Eleonora A. [Noga] Alberti has published versions of *La vuelta del marido* (*í*) and *Landarico*, collected from Eastern informants in Buenos Aires and Asunción (Paraguay). See her "Romances tradicionales en Latinoamérica: Algunos ejemplos sefaradíes y criollos," *Comunidades judías de Latinoamérica (1973−1975)* (Buenos Aires: Comité Judío Americano, Instituto de Ralaciones Humanas, 1975), pp. 252−269.

[17]No ballads have, to our knowledge, been collected in the African settlements. On Sephardic immigration to Rhodesia and South Africa, mostly from the Island of Rhodes, see Marc D. Angel, *The Jews of Rhodes: The History of a Sephardic Community* (New York: Sepher-Hermon Press, 1978), pp. 146, 182; also Reuben Kashani, "Sephardi Community in Capetown, South Africa," *Challenge* (Jerusalem), 3:12 (October 1979), 12.

[18]We know of the existence of some 1,600 ballad texts collected *in situ* in the Eastern communities (counting some 100 Sabra versions recorded in Israel by I. J. Katz, ourselves, and others; but excluding texts provided by Eastern immigrants to Israel); to our knowledge, some 2,363 texts have been collected in Morocco; as contrasted with some 920 Eastern and 56 Moroccan texts collected in the United States and 510 from recent immigrants to Israel (338 Eastern; 172 Moroccan). Such statistics, however, are approximate and, being of necessity incomplete, must be seen as having only doubtful value. We do not know, for example, the statistics of the Moroccan collections of Manuel Alvar, Tomas García Figueras (now housed in the Biblioteca Nacional, Madrid), and Henrietta Yurchenko. On these collections, see M. Alvar, *Poesía tradicional de los judíos españoles* (Mexico City: Porrúa, 1966), p. ix; T. García Figueras, "Romances hispánicos en las juderías de Marruecos," *ABC*, September 24, 1961; H. Yurchenko, "Taping History in Morocco," *The American Record Guide* (New York), 24:4 (December 1957), 130−132, 175. Nor do we know the extent—or present fate—of Alberto Hemsi's unedited Eastern collection. See "Sur le folklore séfardi," *JS*, 18 (April 1959), 794−795. Isaac Levy's unedited collection likewise remains unknown. Moshe Attias refers to various unedited ballad collections that were in his possession. In 1927, Sarah Begas gave him the texts that she had transcribed in Larissa, her birthplace, and Salonika during the 1890s and the early years of the present century. Dr. Samuel Pinto presented in 1957 to Attias a copy of a rich collection of ballads and lyric songs that he had gathered in Sarajevo. Some time after the death of Salomon Israel Cherezli (1937), his son Achinoam gave Attias a selection of traditional poetry found among the posthumous papers of the distinguished lexicographer (see n. 5 above). See M. Attias, *Cancionero judeo-español* (Jerusalem: Centro de Estudios sobre el Judaísmo de Salónica, 1972), pp. 300−301, 323-325, 333,

Judeo-Spanish ballad research in America begins with the *romances* we have annotated in the present edition: 46 texts of Eastern Mediterranean and Moroccan origin, representing 43 different text-types, collected by Professor Maír José Benardete in New York City during the winter of 1922 and spring of 1923.[19] Benardete's pioneering work was to be followed by that of many other collectors. The next attempt to tap the rich and variegated Sephardic ballad resources available in New York[20] was put forward by Federico de Onís who, between 1930 and 1938, made phonograph recordings of North African and Eastern ballads at Columbia University. Starting around 1930, Onís recorded seven *romances* sung by Suzanne (Simy) Nahón de Toledano from Tangier.[21] The Moroccan recordings were followed by others devoted to ballads sung by Eastern (Rhodian and Salonikan) informants in 1933, 1934, 1935, and 1938. In addition to the texts collected from Mrs. Toledano, Onís recorded a total of 22 Eastern Sephardic *romances*. Contemporary with Onís's work were the recordings produced at Barnard College in 1930 (or 1931) by Franz Boas and Zarita Nahón, who collected 15 *romances* (as well as two children's songs, two wedding songs, a lullaby, and an *endecha* [dirge]) also sung by Mrs. Toledano.[22] The early 1930s also saw another important collecting campaign in the Sephardic community of Seattle (Washington): Between 1931 and 1936, Emma Adatto collected ballads, folk-tales (*konsežas*), and proverbs from Turkish and Rhodian informants in Seattle, to form a rich and highly significant body of Judeo-Spanish folk-literature, which, unfortunately, remains largely unedited to this day: 18 *romances* (representing 15 text-types) are included in her M.A. thesis; 28 more texts (= 19 text-types), some of which overlap, with minor variations, the thesis texts, figure in unedited MSS and typescripts; 31 more texts were recorded on phonograph discs at the University of Washington;

---

n. 58; "Çĕrôr rômansôṭ bi-kṭ "y šel Sarayevo," *Shevet va'Am*, 2 (=7) (1973), 295−370: p. 299; and our article (with Iacob M. Hassán), "Un nuevo testimonio del romancero sefardí en el siglo XVIII," *ESef*, 1 (1978), 197−212. Undoubtedly still other unedited collections have escaped our notice.

[19]"Los romances judeo-españoles en Nueva York" (M.A. thesis, Columbia University, 1923).

[20]See Louis M. Hacker, "The Communal Life of the Sephardic Jews in New York City," *Journal of Jewish Communal Service* (New York), 3 (1926), 32−40; Max A. Luria, "Judeo-Spanish Dialects in New York City," *Todd Memorial Volumes: Philological Studies*, II, ed. John D. Fitz-Gerald and Pauline Taylor (New York: Columbia University Press, 1930), 7−16.

[21]See S. G. Armistead and J. H. Silverman (with the collaboration of O. A. Librowicz), *Romances judeo-españoles de Tánger*, collected by Zarita Nahón (Madrid: C.S.M.P., 1977), pp. 24 n. 43, and 229. Some (or all?) of the Toledano recordings may be later than we supposed. One of the discs is dated "May 1936."

[22]See S. G. Armistead, I. J. Katz, and J. H. Silverman, "Judeo-Spanish Folk Poetry from Morocco (The Boas−Nahón Collection)," *YIFMC*, 11 (1979), 59−75.

and nine more are included in the unedited collection of the Archivo Menéndez Pidal in Madrid.[23] On February 18, 1935, Henry V. Besso attended a "Recital de música sefardí" at the Hispanic Institute in New York and obtained the texts of four *romances* sung on that occasion, which he was to publish years later in the *Homenaje a Federico de Onís*.[24]

The years immediately preceding World War II, the unspeakable events of the Holocaust, and the postwar 1940s seemed to mark a complete cessation of research on Sephardic folk-literature in the United States. Only in 1947 did Susan Bassan Warner form a small, but interesting collection of Eastern Sephardic (almost exclusively Salonikan) ballads in her Columbia M.A. thesis.[25] In 1950 David Romey brought together 24 *romances* (plus lyric songs, proverbs, and *konsežas*) from Turkish informants in Seattle, following up the earlier fieldwork of Emma Adatto.[26] At about the same time, Raymond R. MacCurdy revealed the ballad potential of the Atlanta, Georgia, Sephardic community by recording six narrative poems (and two lyric songs) from a Rhodian informant, Mrs. Catina Cohen.[27] In 1952, Denah Levy Lida included Smyrnian versions of *Conde Niño, Muerte del príncipe don Juan, La doncella guerrera*, and *El buceador* in her Ph.D. dissertation on the Izmir dialect of New York.[28] MacCurdy's work in Atlanta was followed up, in the late 1950s, by Isaac Jack Levy, who brought together an abundant corpus of ballads sung and recited by Eastern informants both in Atlanta and in Brooklyn.[29]

Our own field activities, aimed at forming and saving for future generations a massive collection of Sephardic folk-literature, began in Los Angeles in

---

[23]See E. Adatto Schlesinger, "A Study of the Linguistic Characteristics of the Seattle Sefardí Folklore" (M.A. thesis, University of Washington, 1935); also CMP, III, 145–146 (*encuestas* 230–236).

[24]H. V. Besso, "Los sefardíes y el idioma castellano," *RHM*, 34 (1968), 176–194: pp. 188–189.

[25]Susan Bassan [Warner], "Judeo-Spanish Folk Poetry" (M.A. thesis, Columbia University, 1947). Among the apparently unedited *romances* and *romancillos* she cites, we count ten texts from the Salonikan tradition and a fragment from Monastir.

[26]"A Study of Spanish Tradition in Isolation as Found in the Romances, Refranes, and Storied Folklore of the Seattle Sephardic Community" (M.A. thesis, University of Washington, 1950).

[27]Raymond R. MacCurdy and Daniel D. Stanley, "Judaeo-Spanish Ballads from Atlanta, Georgia," *SFQ*, 15 (1951), 221–238.

[28]"El sefardí esmirniano de Nueva York" (Ph.D. diss., Universidad Nacional Autónoma de México, 1952), pp. 63, 64, 67–68, 69–70; on the rare *Buceador*, see our article in *ESef*, 1 (1978), 59–64.

[29]Isaac Jack Levy, "Sephardic Ballads and Songs in the United States: New Variants and Additions" (M.A. thesis, University of Iowa, 1959); also Ralph Tarica, "Sephardic Culture in Atlanta," *South Atlantic Bulletin* (S.A.M.L.A., Chapel Hill, N.C.), 25:4 (March 1960), 1–5. Cf. Itzhak Bar-Lewaw, "Aspectos del judeo-español de las comunidades sefardíes en Atlanta, Ga. y Montgomery, Ala. (EE. UU.)," *XI Congreso Internacional de Lingüística y Filología Románicas: Actas*, 4, 2109–2124: p. 2119.

August 1957. In 1958 and 1959 we extended our work to Seattle, San Francisco, and New York. The most intensive fieldwork in the United States was conducted between 1957 and 1960, though there have also been subsequent recording sessions in Los Angeles (1963), Philadelphia (1969), and New York (1971). As of now, the total number of texts we have recorded in the United States stands at around five hundred (plus many hundreds more collected in Israel and in Morocco, in collaboration with Israel J. Katz). Except for one brief Moroccan interview in Los Angeles (1963), our entire U.S. collection was provided by Eastern singers. A total of 76 informants were interviewed. The texts collected in the United States embody 84 different text-types.[30]

The 1970s have witnessed a surge of interest in all aspects of the Pan-Hispanic *Romancero*.[31] Sephardic ballad studies have recently been favored by the fieldwork of three young scholars: Rina Benmayor, Oro Anahory Librowicz, and Mónica E. Hollander. Working in Los Angeles and Seattle, Rina Benmayor brought together, between November 1972 and June 1973, a splendid collection of some 125 versions, representing 39 different text-types. The collection's special contribution lies in its abundant documentation from the Bosphorus communities, an area largely neglected in earlier explorations.[32] Since 1971, Oro Librowicz has formed a highly significant collection of some 252 ballads from the North African communities and Gibraltar. Derived from 22 different informants in New York, Madrid, Málaga, Caracas, Montreal, Tangier, and Israel, her collection represents 82 different narrative types.[33] The texts recorded in New York (15 *romances*) were sung by an informant from Gibraltar, thus providing knowledge of a heretofore unknown branch of the North African tradition. Mónica Hollander's fieldwork in New York and in

---

[30]See J. H. Silverman, "Hacia un gran romancero sefardí," *El Romancero en la tradición oral moderna*, pp. 31–38; also our *Tres calas en el romancero*, pp. 116–119.

[31]See S. G. Armistead, "A Critical Bibliography of the Hispanic Ballad in Oral Tradition (1971–1979)," *El Romancero hoy: Historia, comparatismo, bibliografía crítica*, ed. S. G. Armistead, A. Sánchez Romeralo, and D. Catalán (Madrid: C.S.M.P. and University of California, 1979), pp. 199–310; S. G. Armistead, "*Romancero* Studies (1977–1979)," *La Corónica*, 8:1 (Fall 1979), 57–66.

[32]"Romances judeo-españoles de Oriente recogidos en la Costa Occidental de los Estados Unidos" (Ph.D. diss., University of California, Berkeley, 1974); revised, with the addition of numerous texts, as *Romances judeo-españoles de Oriente: Nueva recolección*, Madrid: C.S.M.P., 1979. See also Rina Benmayor, "Oral Narrative and the Comparative Method: *The Judeo-Spanish Ballad Chapbooks of Yacob Abraham Yoná*," *RPh*, 31 (1977–1978), 501–521; idem, "A Greek *Tragoúdi* in the Repertoire of a Judeo-Spanish Ballad Singer," *HR*, 46 (1978), 475–479; idem, "Un texto sefardí oriental del *Cautivo del renegado*," *ESef*, 1 (1978), 139–141.

[33]See the publications cited in n. 6; also "Florilegio de romances sefardíes de la diáspora: Breve panorama de una colección judeo-malagueña," *El Romancero hoy: Nuevas fronteras*, ed. A. Sánchez Romeralo, D. Catalán, and S. G. Armistead (Madrid: C.S.M.P. and University of California, 1979), pp. 91–97.

Montevideo (Uruguay), between December 1972 and November 1973, has produced a collection of some 80 *romance* texts, reflecting 35 different text-types, recorded from 21 different informants originally from Yugoslavia, Greece, and Turkey. Well over half of the versions were collected in the United States.[34]

Sephardic ballad fieldwork in the United States has produced notable results. Many hundreds of texts which would otherwise have vanished without a trace have been saved from oblivion. Yet much more remains to be done and many communities have yet to be explored: Highland Park (New Jersey), Cleveland (Ohio), Indianapolis (Indiana), Chicago (Illinois), Montgomery (Alabama), Miami (Florida), and Portland (Oregon), among others, all have Sephardic communities that await exploration.[35] As Sephardic speech and folklore retreat

[34]See the dissertation cited in n. 15; also "Romances judeo-españoles de Oriente recogidos en Montevideo y Nueva York," *El Romancero hoy: Nuevas fronteras*, pp. 99–104. There are other instances of Sephardic ballad collecting in the United States. William Samuelson of San Antonio (Texas) has formed an interesting collection of *romances* from Turkey, though none of the songs published in his "Romances and Songs of the Sephardim," *The Sephardi Heritage: Essays on the History and Cultural Contribution of the Jews of Spain and Portugal*, ed. Richard D. Barnett, (New York: Ktav, 1971), I, 527–551, can be classed as a *romance*. Recently, Robin Greenstein included two *romances* (*Landarico* and *Sentenciado del bajá*) in *La Serena: A Collection of Ladino Songs* ([Washington, D.C.], American Jewish Congress, Martin Steinberg Center, 1979).

[35]Concerning Sephardic communities in the United States and elsewhere in the world, see David Ahiod, "Judaísmo sobre las orillas del Bósforo," *Voz Sefaradí*, 1:2 (July 1966), 7–10; Marc D. Angel, "The Sephardim of the United States: An Exploratory Study," *American Jewish Yearbook* (New York and Philadelphia), 74 (1973), 77–138; idem, *The Jews of Rhodes*, pp. 146–148; M. J. Benardete, *Hispanic Culture and Character of the Sephardic Jews* (New York: Hispanic Institute, 1952), pp. 134–151; idem, *Hispanismo de los sefardíes levantinos* (Madrid: Aguilar, 1963), pp. 154–174; Joan Dash, "Sephardim: A Modern Door to Fifteenth-Century Spain," *Américas*, 17:10 (October 1965), 8–14; Leonard Plotnick, "The Sephardim of New Lots: Self-Containment and Expansion," *Commentary*, 25:1 (January 1958), 28–35; Allen H. Podet and Dan Chasan, "Heirs to a Noble Past: Seattle's Storied Sephardic Jews," *Seattle Magazine* 4:38 (May 1967), 40–48; David de Sola Pool, Raphael Patai, and Abraham Lopes Cardozo, *The World of the Sephardim* (New York: Herzl Press, 1960); Stephen Stern, "The Sephardic Jewish Community of Los Angeles: A Study in Folklore and Ethnic Identity" (Ph.D. diss. Indiana University, 1977); Vicki Tamir, *Bulgaria and Her Jews: The History of a Dubious Symbiosis* (New York: Sepher-Hermon Press, 1979). Max Vorspan and Lloyd P. Gartner, *History of the Jews of Los Angeles* (Philadelphia: J.P.S.A., 1970) includes little information on the Sephardim. See, however, pp. 116, 261–262, 321 n. 31, and 345 n. 12.

Among the papers of Américo Castro we found an interesting article by R. Marín entitled "Los sefarditas de Manila," published in *Democracia Española* (Manila, November 30, 1937). Marín noted that there was a large Sephardic colony of Turkish origin that had been established in the city around 1913. In describing a warm reception that the Sephardim had prepared for Antonio Jaén, the Spanish Consul-General, he mentioned that there was much singing of "viejas melodías españolas" and "viejos romances castellanos." One can only lament that no one was there to copy down the precious versions sung in Manila that afternoon in honor of Sr. Jaén and "la España doliente, liberal, democrática y republicana." For another example of a regrettably lost opportunity to transcribe Sephardic ballads from the oral tradition, see Joseph H. Silverman, "La contaminación como arte en un romance de Tánger," *El Romancero hoy: Poética*, ed. D. Catalán, S. G.

before the irresistible onslaught of the English language and modern American mass-media culture, the urgency of renewed efforts toward further fieldwork becomes patently clear. Without doubt the next few years will see the irretrievable disappearance of whatever now remains to be saved.[36]

Maír José Benardete's pioneering work in New York City—the first Sephardic ballad-collecting campaign ever undertaken in the United States—is important for a number of reasons, above and beyond the mere chronological fact of having captured a sample of the tradition almost a decade before the work of any other American collector. Benardete is also the only fieldworker to date to have attempted an extensive survey of both branches of the Sephardic tradition from the vantage point of the American immigrant communities. All of us who worked subsequently have, in our American fieldwork, concentrated our efforts on either Eastern or Moroccan informants. Benardete, on the other hand, cast a wide net and came up with a number of rare text-types, some of which have not been recorded again in the U.S. communities—or, at best, have only been recorded in single texts or exiguous fragments. Such are numbers (1) *Destierro del Cid + Quejas de Jimena*; (3) *Sueño de doña Alda + Melisenda insomne*; (8) *Expulsión de los judíos de Portugal*; (31) *Rapto*; (32) *Forzador*; (38) *Pozo airón*; and (39) *Sierpe del río*. As a representative of the Salonikan tradition, (17) *Tarquino y Lucrecia* should also be noted for its rarity and the same can be said of (20*B*) *Don Bueso y su hermana*, which, in its archaic hexasyllabic form, is now scarcely heard in the Moroccan tradition. Among Benardete's texts there are also a number that offer significant new insights into the variegated traditional life of the ballads in question. His *Sueño de doña Alda* (no. 3) is unique in preserving a vestige of the original bird imagery of the protagonist's ominous dream. His no. 19, *Hermanas reina y cautiva*, allows us to document for the first time in the Moroccan tradition the use of the "euphe-

---

Armistead, A. Sánchez Romeralo (Madrid: C.S.M.P. and University of California, 1979), pp. 29–37; 35–36 n. 6.

[36]On the twentieth-century crisis of Sephardic culture, see M. J. Benardete, "Cultural Erosion among the Hispano-Levantine Jews," *Homenaje a Millás-Vallicrosa*, 2 vols. (Barcelona: C.S.I.C., 1954), I, 125–154; Henry V. Besso, "Decadencia del judeo-español: Perspectivas para el futuro," *Actas del Primer Simposio de Estudios Sefardíes*, ed I. M. Hassán et al. (Madrid: C.S.I.C., 1970), pp. 249–261 and the discussion of his paper on pp. 414–426; Denah Lida, "The Vanishing Sephardim," *JS*, no. 24 (July 1962), 1035–1040, 1048; Juan Octavio Prenz, "Vicisitudes del judeo-español de Bosnia," *Románica*, 1 (1968), 163–173; Sephiha, *L'Agonie*, passim; and for additional references, our *Tres calas en el romancero*, p. 141 n. 39.

Jacob Glantz—a pioneer of Mexican Yiddish poetry—once observed with undisguised melancholy: "We Yiddish poets are the loneliest in the world, poets without young readers." Elderly Sephardic ballad singers might respond: "We Sephardic balladeers are the loneliest in the world, singers without young listeners."

mistic third person'' in referring to tragic events. Benardete's Moroccan *Vuelta del marido* (*é*) no. 22, attests to an uncommon migratory epilogue. No. 24, *Diego León*, offers a singular contamination from the rare *Mal casamiento impedido*. His unique Salonikan version of *El conde Alarcos* (no. 27) takes the narrative one stage further than any other variant published to date. No. 28*A*, a fragment of *La mala suegra*, offers a notable example of the interaction of ballads and proverbs; and Benardete's version of *El rapto* (no. 31) offers readings that help us to bridge the gap between the modern North African tradition and the song recorded by Lope de Vega.

In the present edition, we have maintained the normative orthography used in the original thesis. Contaminated texts containing more than one narrative type, which in Benardete's thesis were separated into their various components, have been reunited here. In the section devoted to English abstracts and bibliography, we have attempted to draft summaries based on all published texts known to us and on every available unpublished version as well. The abstracts follow those included in CMP but, in every case, they have been considerably amplified with numerous details produced by a more exhaustive consultation of edited and unedited materials. Each abstract is specific to the subtradition—Eastern or Moroccan—to which the texts edited here belong. The bibliography strives to be exhaustive for both branches of the Sephardic *romancero*, in that we have attempted to list all versions, both published and unedited, which have been consulted or are known to us. Following the Sephardic listings in the individual bibliographies of each text-type, references, where pertinent, are provided to the most important collections in the modern Castilian, Portuguese, Catalan, and Hispano-American traditions; then, to earlier (fifteenth- to seventeenth-century) evidence, if it exists; and, finally, to any known analogues in other European traditions, using in each case the fundamental research instruments for each category. In these individual bibliographies, Eastern texts bear no introductory sign; a single slash (/) marks references to Moroccan versions; two (//) indicate Peninsular and Hispano-American collections; three (///) introduce early (fifteenth- to seventeenth-century) texts; and four (////) mark analogues in other European traditions. A thematic classification (correlated to CMP), a general bibliography, indexes of informants, ballad titles, and first verses, and a glossary of dialect forms have also been provided.

It is a pleasure to acknowledge the generous support of the Memorial Foundation for Jewish Culture and the Committee on Research of the University of California at Santa Cruz in the preparation and printing of this volume.

James Kubeck was very helpful in submitting our work to the University of California Press. Deirdre Jackson, Judith Pepper, and Diane Roberts provided excellent editorial assistance and typing. Our greatest debt of gratitude is, of course, to Professor Maír J. Benardete for granting us the opportunity to prepare this edition of his precious ballad collection.

S.G.A. and J.H.S.

Philadelphia and Santa Cruz
February 1980

THE BALLADS

1

EL DESTIERRO DEL CID (á-o) +
LAS QUEJAS DE JIMENA (á-e)
(MP 5/A9 + MP 3/A3)

Tetuán

   —¿Dónde habéis estado, el Cidi,   que en las cortes no hubéis estado?

2 Viñas y castíos, el Cidi,   me han dicho que habéis ganado.

    Parte con el Conde Adoña,   que es pobre y bien gigante.

4 —Dale de la tuya, el rey,   que la habéis ganado.

    Los míos son ganados   en sangre de gente noble.

6 —Desterrarte yo a ti, el Cidi,   por mis tierras un año.

    —Irme de tus civdades,   mala y de mala gente.

8 Irme a las de mi padre,   buena y de buena gente.—

    La cabeza entre los hombros   y al suelo se la ronjara.

10 —Justicia, justicia, señor rey,   si me la quizieres darme.

   . . . .   Veo hoy quién mató a mi padre.

12 Me come mis palomitas,   cuantas he en mi palomare.

    El rey que esto no juzga   no debía de reinare,

14 ni comer pan a mantele,   ni con la reina durmire.

    —Haremos un gran contrato,   Ximena, si a ti te plaze,

16 de cazarte con el Cidi,   sabiendo que tanto vale.

    Y alegre salid, Ximena,   de sus palacios reale.—

18 Otro día la mañana,   las ricas bodas s'armaron.

2a   Viñas: *read* Villas.
6a   Desterrarte: *read* Desterrarte he.
7a,8b Irme: *read* Irme he.
14a   mantele: *read* manteles.
17b   reale: *read* reales.

2

ALMERIQUE DE NARBONA (*i*) + RONCES-VALLES (*i*) + LAS BODAS EN PARIS (*i*) (MP 20/B8 + MP 20/B3 + MP 95/M14)

Salonika

Aquel conde y aquel conde,   en la mar sea su fín,
2 armó naves y galeras,   para Francia quijo ir.
Las armó de todo punto   y las echó dientro el sanjí.
4 —Atrás, atrás, los mis franceses,   no me dex vergüenza ansí.
Si el gran Francés lo sabe,   a Francia no mos dex a ir.
6 No mos dan pan a comere,   ni con las damas dormir.
A la tornada qu'atornó   mataron setenta mil,
8 aparte de chicos y pequeños   . . . .
—Si vos plaze el buen conde,   yo vos iré a servir;
10 el día para la meza,   la noche para dormir.
Marido en viaje tengo,   lonje está para venir.
12 Una esfuegra vieja tengo,   no ve la luz del candil.
Un esfuegro viejo tengo,   malo está para murir.
14 Dos hijicos chicos tengo,   no lo saben dezir.—
La emburujó en mantil de oro,   de afuera le quedó el chapín.
16 En medio del camino,   encontró con Amadí.
—¿Qué yeváx aquí, el conde,   y qué yeváx aquí?
18 —Yevo un paxarico de oro,   que agüera lo aferí.
—No lo conocí en el garbe,   ni menos en el vestir.
20 La conocí en el chapín de oro,   que yinda ayer lo merquí.
Esto que oyó el buen conde,   dexó todo y se echó a fuir.
22 —No vos fuigáx, el buen conde,   ni vos queráx fuir.
Esto no es la vuestra culpa,   sino es que yo la buxquí.

5*b*   *read* dexa ir.

3

EL SUEÑO DE DOÑA ALDA (*á-e*) +
MELISENDA INSOMNE (*á-e*)
(MP 21/B6 + MP 28/B17)

Salonika

En París está Duña Alda,   la hija del imperalde,
2 con trescientas damas con eya,   todas son de alto linaje.
No vos toméx maraviya,   que todas oficio hazen.
4 Las ciento filaban perla   y las cientos oro majare
y las ciento filaban sirma   para Duña Alda labrare.
6 Noche buena, noche buena,   noche era de anamorarse,
no durmió la Merizelda,   la hija del imperalde,
8 de amores del conde Argile,   el su amigo caronale,
vueltas daba por la cama,   como da el pexe en la mare.
10 Se echó de la cama abaxo,   como quien se echa en la mare.
Se echó de la cama abaxo,   para sus donzeyas andare:
12 —Si durmíx, las mis donzellas,   si durmíx, arecordarme.—
Todas cayaron a una,   ninguna respuesta hay dare.
14 —Un esfueño m'hay soñado;   en bien me lo hay de soltare.—
Allí se topó una vieja,   vieja de antigüedade:
16 —Digáx el esfueño, señora;   yo vo lo hay de soltare.
—Yo, por los campos d'Alsume,   una galza vide volare.
18 —La galza sox vos, mi señora,   y el conde vuestro amigo caronale.
Andavos para la caxa,   para la caxa d'anxugare,
20 a meter vos camisa de seda,   sirma y perla al cavesale.—
Ya se hue la Merizelda,   para la caxa d'anxugare,
22 a meterse camisa de seda,   sirma y perla y cavesale.
Cien damas se la lavraron   a la oriya de la mare;
24 y otras cien se la cuzieron   mañanica de San Juare;
y las otras cien iban con eya,   la iyan acompañare.

4

GAIFEROS JUGADOR (*á-e*)
(B15)

Salonika

Por palacio de Carlo   non pasan sinon jugare.
2 No jugan plata ni oro,   sinon vías y civdades.
Ganó Carlo a Gaifero   sus vías y sus civdades.
4 Ganó Carlo a Gaifero   y a la su mujer reale.
Más valía a pedrerla,   pedrerla que non ganare.
6 —Subrino, el mi sobrino,   el mi sobrino caronale,
yo vos creí chiquitico,   el Diez te hizo baragane.
8 El te dio barbica roxa   y en tu puerpo fuerza grande.
Yo vos di a Blancaniña   por mujer y por iguale.
10 Fuitex un hombre covado,   vola dexatex yevare;
un día, estando en la milsa,   en el vergel de vuestro padre,
12 cojendo rozas y flores,   mañana de San Juare.
Maldición vos echo, el mi sobrino,   si no la vax a buxcare.
14 Por los caminos que vax,   no topéx ni vino ni pane,
ni menos dinero en bolsa,   para el camino gastare.
16 No dex cebada a la mula,   ni carne cruda al gavilane.
La mujer que vos tuvierex   non vos guadre crueldade.
18 Los hijos que vos pariere   no vos conoscan por padre.

5

ROSAFLORIDA Y MONTESINOS (*i-a*)
(MP 26/B20)

Tangier

En un castío está, un castío, y aquel castío luzero,
2 rodeado está de almenas, del oro de la Turquía.
Entre almenas y almenas, está una piedra zafira.
4 Dientro estaba una donzeya, se yamaba Rozaflorida.
Ya la media noche, gritos da Rozaflorida.
6 Namoróse de Montizinos, de oídos y non de vista.
Y hasia la medianoche, gritos dio Rozaflorida:
8 —Si nos aljadra aquí alguno, que me tenga manzía.
Que me yeven estas cartas a Francia la bien guarida.
10 Se los den a Montezino y al bien que yo más quería.
Le regalo sus caminos en asufare y piedras finas.
12 La daré cien negritos, que le guizen en la cozina.
Le daré clavo y canela, con que sabore su comida.
14 Le daré los cien negritos, vestidos a la Turquía.
Le daré oro y plata, con que negocie toda su vida.
16 De encima de todo esto, mi cuerpo más valía.
Si no me quiziera a mí, le daré a una hermana niña.
18 Eya me gana en la hermozura; yo la gano en galentía.—
Eyos en estas palabras, Montezino yegaría.
20 —¿Hijo de quién sois, mi vida, hijo de quién sois, mi alma?
—Hijo soy de un carbonero, que mi padre lo hazía,
22 . . . . y mi tío lo vendía.—
Como eso oyó Rozaflorida y en desmayo cayería.
24 —No vos desmayes, mi vida, no vos desmayes, mi alma.
Hijo soy del rey de Francia, nieto del rey de Turquía.—
26 Y otro día en la mañana, ricas bodas s'armaron.

7a *orig.* Ya se a la m.
22b *orig.* me

6

JUAN LORENZO (*á*)
(MP 12/C2)

Salonika

    —Jan Nolencio, ¿quién te hizo tanto mal?
2 ¿Ánde está tu gentileza,   como esfullía es de estar?
    —Por tener mujer hermoza,   el rey me quere matar.
4 Yo estando en la mi puerta,   con la mi mujer real,
    sonando la mi virgüela   y mis hijos al son bailán,
6 vide venir gentíos de gente,   gente eran sin asumar.
    El corasón me lo dixera   que era el rey de Portugar.
8 Yo me echí la capa al hombro   y lo fui a saludar.
    Ya me lo truxé en caza,   presto le di almorzar . . .

2*b*   esfullía es: *read* esfuelíaš.

7

LA MUERTE DEL DUQUE DE GANDÍA (*í-a*)
(MP 14/C12)

7*A*. Gelibolu

 Más arriba y más arriba,   en la ciudad de Mesina,
2 ayí había un pexcadore,   pexcando su probería.
 Vido venir tres en cabayo,   haziendo gran polvería.
4 Una cosa yevaban en hombros;   de lexos no se vería.
 Vinieron cerca del río,   a la mar lo echarían.
6 Echó gancho y ganchera,   por ver lo que salía.
 Le salió duque de oro,   hijo del rey parecía.
8 Camisa de holanda yevaba,   cabezón de perla fina;
 aniyo yeba en el dedo,   cien pobres ricos hazía.
10 Pregoneros por las plazas,   hijo del rey quién vería:
 —Si me lo trayen bivo,   hombre grande los hazía.
12 Y se me lo trayen muerto,   un gran pexquek les daría.

7*B*. Çanakkale (Dardanelles)

 Más arriba y más arriba,   en la ciudad de Mesina,
2 vide venir tres en cabayo,   haziendo gran polvería.
 Coza yevaban en el hombro,   de enfrente no se vería.
4 Cerca del río vinieron,   a la mar lo echarían.
 Ayí había pexcadores,   pexcando su povrería.
6 Echó gangos y gangeros,   por ver lo que le salría.
 Le salió un dulque de oro,   hijo del rey parecía.

6*a* gangos, gangeros: *read* ganchos, gancheros.

8 Camiza colanda yeva,   cavesal de sirma y perla;
    aniyo yeva en el dedo,   cien pobres ricos hazía.
10 Estas palabras diziendo, ...
    pregoneros por las plazas,   hijo del rey quién vería:
12 —El que me lo traye vivo,   su bacxíx le daría.
    El que me lo traye muerto,   su paga yo le daría.—
14 Estas palabras diciendo,   la romanza s'acabaría.

8*a*   colanda: *read* holanda.

7C. Izmir

    Cuando los ricos mancebos   salen a cabayería,
2 con estreyas en los cielos   y el lunar esclarecía,
    vido venir tres en cabayo,   haziendo gran polvería.
4 Viéndose cerca del río,   al río lo echarían.
    Un baque daba el río,   que el río temblaría.
6 Pexcador que está pexcando,   pexcando su probería,
    echó gancho y gancheras,   por ver lo que le salía.
8 Le salió un dunque de oro,   hijo del rey parecía.
    Camiza d'holanda yeva,   cavesón de sirma y perla,
10 aniyo yeva en su dedo,   cien pobres ricos azía;
    un calpáx yeva en el hombro,   cien ciudades más valía.
12 Pregoneros quita el rey,   el hijo quién vería:
    Todo el que se lo trae vivo,   gran pexquéx le daría.
14 Todo el que se lo trae muerto,   hombre grande lo haría.

8

LA EXPULSIÓN DE LOS JUDÍOS DE PORTUGAL
(í-o)
(MP 13/C13)

Salonika

  ¡Diez del cielo, Diez del cielo,   Diez del cielo, hazed conmigo!
2 Que éramos las tres hermanas,   hija del rey dolorido.
  Las dos ya están cazadas;   la chica no le dan marido.
4 . . . .   Que de oro está cozido;
  sinon por falta de ventura,   que del cielo no la ha venido.
6 Estas palabras diziendo,   ḥaberjís que le han venido,
  que se le murió la hermana;   en su lugar la han metido.

2*b*   hija: *read* hijas.
7*b*   *orig.* en metido.

9

LA MUERTE DEL PRÍNCIPE DON JUAN (*á-a*)
(MP 15/C14)

9*A*. Salonika

    Malo está el hijo del reye,   malo está que no salva.
2 Siete dotores lo miran,   los mijores de Granada.
    Siete dotores lo miran,   ninguno le haze nada.
4 Inda manca de venire   el de la barba envicitada.
    Estas palabras deziendo,   el doctor que arrivara.
6 Subido en mula prieta,   rizá de oro en su garganta.
    Se le asentó en la cabesera,   el pulso ya le tocaba:
8 —Tres horas tiene de vida,   hora y media hay pasado.
    En esta horica y media,   hazelde bien por su alma.—
10 Ya viene la madre amarga,   descalsa y descabeñada.
    —¿Dónde veníx, la su madre,   descalsa y descabeñada?
12 —Vengo de arrogar al Dio   que te alze de esta cama.
    —Si de esta cama me alza,   con un ataúd de oro;
14 si de esta cama me alza   y una rica mortaja.
    —Apartad, la buena gente,   que pasa la malograda.
16 Cuando ya es que lo pasan,   vaya dando la campana.

9*B*. Izmir

    Malo estaba el buen reye,   malo está que s'alaba.
2 Siete doctores lo rijen,   de ninguna repuesta daba.
    Siete mulas y cavayos   por el camino dexaras.

1*b*   s'alaba: *read* no salvaba.

26

4　A la entrada de la puerta,　　la mula ya reventaba:
　—¿Qué dezíx, el buen reye,　　este mal qu'el Dio le daba?
6　—Tres horas tiene de vida,　　hora y media ya es pasada.
　—Si la reina pare hijo,　　seya reina encoronada.
8　Si la reina pare hija,　　seya reina endesdechada.

10

EL NACIMIENTO Y VOCACIÓN DE ABRAHAM
(strophic)
(MP 30/E3)

Salonika

   La mujer de Teraḥ   —   quedó preñada.
2 Día de cada día,   le preguntaba:
   —¿De qué yeváx la cara   tan demudada?
4 O estabax ḥazina,   o estabax preñada.
   —Ni estó ḥazina,   ni estó preñada.—
6 Eya se lo sabía,   el bien que tenía.
   Se fue por estos campos,   por ayí piedrida.
8 Topó una meará,   ayí se entraría.
   Ayí le parería   al señor de Abraham.
10 Y al ocho de la tripa: . . . .
   —Andavos, la mi madre,   andavos d'acá.
12 Que mi señor es Teraḥ,   vos querrá matar.
   Después de quince días,   le salió a buxcar.
14 Lo topó paseando   por la meará.
   En la mano derecha,   una guimará.
16 —¿Qué buxcáx, la mi madre,   qué buxcas acá?
   —Una joya preciosa,   que dexí acá.
18 —Ya vola comería   una ḥayá.—
   Esto sentió la madre,   se metió a yorar.
20 —No yoréx, la mi madre,   ni queréx yorar.
   Que yo so vuestro hijo,   el señor de Abram.—
22 Grande ziḥud tuvo   el señor de Abram.
   Que por él conocimos   al Dio de Abram.

10a Y al ocho: *read* Ya lo echó.

11

EL SACRIFICIO DE ISAAC (*á-o*)
(MP 31/E5)

Tetuán

   —Dame a tu hijo, Abraham,   y a tu hijo Isaac corado.—
2 Para cumplirle las diez,   grande demanda l'había mandado.
   —Ya sabes tú, Abraham,   que tu hijo Isaac le quiero corbán.
4 Y en el monte de Sinai   y ayí le representarás.—
   Ya viene Abraham   a yevar a Isaac corado.
6 —Vamos conmigo, Isaac,   que del cielo es mandado.—
   Se pararon en un monte,   de leña le había cargado.
8 —¿Qué vas hacer con esta leña, mi padre,   que yevas tan cargado?
   —Para ponerlo en el monte, ...
10 Isaac, ataparte los ojos,   porque del cielo es mandado.
   Tú sos el cabrito, mi hijo,   que es corbán para Dios.
12 —Padre, ataime las manos,   padre, ataime bien los ojos.
   Con la furia de la muerte,   no vos vea mal airado.—
14 Abraham tomó el puñal   y al cuello se le había puesto.
   Salió una voz de los cielos,   ya Abraham había yamado.
16 —Tate, tate tú, Abraham,   no mates a Isaac corado.
   Porque Dios de los cielos,   ya te tiene probado.—
18 Ayí s'aljadró un mejatré   y a Sara se lo fue a contar:
   —Si supieras tú, Sara,   lo que por ti hay pasado.
20 Umá Abraham tu marido,   matara a Isaac corado.—
   Como esto oyó Sara,   muerta quedó en desmayo.
22 Con el mismo mejatré,   a Abraham se le fue a contar:
   —Si supieras tú, Abraham,   lo que por ti hay pasado.

1*b*, 5*b*, 16*b*, 20*b* corado: *read* honrado.

24 Umá Sara tu mujer,   muerta quedó en un desmayo.—
    Ya sale el padre y el hijo   descalzos y encapiados.
26 Y en el campo de Hebrón,   ayí la habían enterrado.
    Lo que había de morir Isaac,   murió la su madre.

12

EL ROBO DE DINA (ó)
(MP 32/E7)

Salonika

   Se pasea las doje flores,   entre en medio una conchá.
2 Dixo la conchá a las flores: —Hoy es día de pasear.—
   Se pasea la linda Dina   por los campos del rey Hamor.
4 A favor de sus doje hermanos,   caminaba sin temor.
   Arrimóse a una tienda,   pensando que no hay varón.
6 Visto la hubiera visto   Xehem, hijo del rey Hamor.
   Ayegóse para eya,   tres palabricas le habló.
8 —Linda sox, la linda Dina,   sin afeite y sin color.
   Lindos son vuestros ermanos,   la flor vos yevatex vos.
10 —Si son lindos y non son lindos,   a mí que me lo guadre el Dio.—
   Ayegóse más a eya,   hizo lo que non es razón.
12 Se esparte la linda Dina,   se va a pasear ande su señor.
   A solombra del tejado,   a que no la enfaniara el sol.
14 Su padre, desque la vido,   a recibirla salió:
   —¿Quén vos demudó la cara   y quén vos demudó la color?
16 O vola demudó el aire,   o vola emfanió el sol.
   —Ni me la demudó el aire,   ni me la emfanió el sol.
18 Me la demudó un muchachico,   Xehem, hijo del rey Hamor.—
   Estas palabricas diziendo,   cazamenteros le mandó.

13*b*   enfaniara: *read* empañara.
16*b*, 17*b* emfanió: *read* empañó.

31

13

TAMAR Y AMNÓN (*á-a*)
(MP 37/E17)

Tangier

> Un hijo tiene el rey David, que por nombre Ablón se yama.
> 2 Namoróse de Tamar, aunque era su propia hermana.
> Fuertes fueron los amores, malo cayó echado en cama.
> 4 Un día por la mañana, su padre ya vele entrar.
> —¿Qué tienes y tú, Ablón, hijo mío y de mi alma?
> 6 —Malo estoy yo, el rey mi padre, malo estoy y no como nada.
> —¿Qué comerás tú, Ablón, hijo mío y de mi alma?
> 8 ¿Qué comerás tú, Ablón, pechuga de una pava?
> —Yo la comeré, el rey mi padre, si Tamar me la guizare.
> 10 —Yo se lo diré a Tamar, que te la guize y te la traiga.
> —Si fué cosa que viniere, venga sola y sin compaña.—
> 12 Ellos en estas palabras, Tamar por la puerta entrara.
> —¿Qué tienes tú, Ablón, hermano mío y de mi alma?
> 14 —De tus amores, Tamar, malo estoy echado en cama.
> —Si de mis amores estás malo, que no te levantes de la cama.—
> 16 Tendióle la mano al pecho y a la cama la ronjara.
> Triste saliera Tamar, triste saliera y mal airada.
> 18 Y en meatad de aquel camino, con Absalón se encontrara.
> —¿Qué tienes y tú, Tamar, hermana mía y de mi alma?
> 20 —Umá Ablón tu hermano, me quitó mi honra y fama.
> —No esté de nada, Tamar, no esté de nada, mi alma.
> 22 Antes que araye el sol, su sangre será regada.

4*b* ya vele entrar: *read* y a verle entrara.
21*a* No esté de nada: *read* No se te dé nada.

14

BLANCAFLOR Y FILOMENA (é-a)
(MP 100/F1)

14A. Salonika

Muerto va el hijo del reye, muerto va por Felismena.
2 Siyó mula y cabayo y se iría para la guerra.
 A la tornada qu'atornó, se va para ande la suegra:
4 —¿Qué hazíax, la mi suegra? —Vos, mi yerno, en bien veneríax.
 ¿Qué hazía la mi hija y la mi hija, qué hiziera?
6 —Preñada está de ocho mezes, sola está en tierras ajenas.
 Mucho me arrogó y me dixo, si se puede venir eya.
8 Si eya no podía venire, que me diera a Felismena.
 —De dar, vola do, mi yerno, como hija mía y vuestra.—
10 Ya siyó mula y cabayo, barabar anduvieran.
 Por en medio del camino, de amores le acometiera.
12 —Vos sox el mi cuñado; a qué güerco paresierax.—
 —Se echó de[1] cabayo abaxo; le cortó media algüenga.

14B. Izmir

Muerto está el hijo del rey, muerto está por Felismení.
2 Ya se viste, ya se arma, para la guerra ya partió.
 A la buelta de la guerra, ande la esḥuegra ya entró.
4 —Vengas en buena hora, yerno. —Buena hora me tenga, mi
  esfuegra.
 —¿Ánde dexates a mi hija en ciudades ajenas?
6 —Preñadica de ocho mezes, vine a tomalda a eya.
 Si eya no puede venir, a Felismení me la da.

8   —A Felismení te la daré,   como una hermana vuestra.—
    Ya se viste, ya se arma,   adelante la metió.
10 Siete civdades caminaron,   siete lengua[s] le habló.
    A la civdad de al cabo,   media lengua le cortó.
12 A querer y no querer,   una noche durmió con él.
    Por ay pasa un viejizico,   a Felismení conoció.
14 ¡Malaña tripa de madre   que a su hija la fió!
    Por ser hijo del rey,   ¿a qué güerco pareció?
16 La toma del brasico;   ande la madre se la yevó.
    La madre, que la ve venir,   ya cayó y se desmayó.
18 —Tomalda a Felismení,   asentalda en el cantón.
    Por ser hijo del rey,   ¿a qué güerco pareció?

15

HERO Y LEANDRO (ó) +
LA MALCASADA DEL PASTOR (ó)
(MP 41/F2 + MP 72/L8)

Izmir

   Tres hermanicas eran,   tres hermanicas son.
2 Las dos están cazadas,   la chica en pedrición.
   El padre, con vergüenza,   a Rodes la mandó.
4 En medio del camino,   castiyo le fraguó,
   de piedra menudica,   corral al rededor;
6 ventanas por los mares,   que no suba varón.
   El varón, que ya lo supo,   a nadar ya se echó.
8 Sus brasos hizo remos,   su puerpo navegó.
   Nadando y navegando,   al lugar ya arrivó.
10 Echó sus entrensados,   arriba lo subió.
   Le lavó piezes y manos,   l'agua se bebió.
12 Le quitó y a comeres   pexcado con limón.
   Le quitó y a beberes   vino de treinta y dos.
14 Le quitó y mezeliques   almendricas de Estambol.
   En medio de los comeres,   agua le demandó.
16 Agua no había en caza,   a la fuente la enbió.
   Al son de los tres chorricos,   la niña se durmió.
18 Por ayí pasó un cabayero,   tres bezicos le dio;
   uno de cara en cara   y otro de corasón.
20 Al bezico de al cabo,   la niña se espertó.
   —¿Qué hizites, cabayero,   matada merezco yo,
22 matada con un puño,   que dos no quero yo.
   —No t'espantes, mi querida,   que'l tu amor so yo.—
24 La tomó del brasico,   a casa se la yevó.

16

EL ROBO DE ELENA (*á-o*)
(MP 43/F5)

Salonika

Estábase la reina Izela   en su bastidor labrando,
2 algujica de oro en mano,   un pendón de amor labrando.
Por ayí pasó Parisí,   el su lindo enamorado.
4 —Para este puerpo, Parisí,   ¿qué oficio habréx tomado?
—Mercader, la mi señora,   mercader y escribano.
6 Tres naves tengo en el golfo,   cargadas de oro brocado.
En la nave que yo vengo,   había un rico manzano.
8 Echa manzanas de amores   invierno y enverano.
—Si es esto verdad, Parisí,   gloria es de lo contare.
10 Si os plazía, Parisí,   vos iré a vijitaros.
—Venid en buena hora, reina Izelda,   vos y vuestro reinado.
12 —Estéx en buena hora, Parisí,   vos y el vuestro palacio.—
De que la vido de enfrente,   armó velas y alevantó gancho.
14 Cuando la vido a su lado,   abrió puertas del palacio.
—¿Ónde está el manzano, ...
16 que echa manzanas de amores   envierno y enverano?
Me engañatex vos, Parisí,   con vuestro hablar delicado.

3*a*,   *et passim* Parisí: *read* Parisi.

36

17

TARQUINO Y LUCRECIA (á-a)
(MP 45/F7)

Salonika

   Aquel rey de los romanzos,   que Tarquino que se yamaba,
2 vistióse hombre de camino,   por la puerta le pasa.
   Ducquerencia, que lo vido,   gran plazer tomó su alma.
4 Quitóle gaína en cena   y cama d'oro donde lo echara.
   A la fin de la media noche,   Tarquino que se despertare.
6 Metióle puño en sus pechos,   por ver si se despertare.
   Despertóse Ducquerencia   con gran temblor en su alma.
8 —¿Quén es éste el que bate   tales horas por la mi cama?
   —Vuestro amor, Ducquerencia,   que le hazéx penar su alma.
10 Si tú esto me hazes,   medio reinado por tu grado.
   Si tú esto a mí no me hazes,   con la espada te cortare.
12 Si tú esto a mí no me hazes, ...
   yo te echaré fama por Roma   que yo durmir con ti en una cama.
14 —Más vale murir con honra   y non vivir desfamada.

2a *orig.* vistróse.

37

18

VIRGILIOS (é)
(MP 46/F8)

Salonika

Traisión a Don Virgile,   por los palacios del reye,
2 por amare a una señora,   por amarla y bien quererle.
El rey, estando en la misa,   vido venir a una mujere,
4 vestida entera de luto   de la cabesa a los pies.
Demandó el rey a su gente   quén era esta mujer.
6 —Mujer era de Don Virgile,   que aquí en presión los tenéx;
en presio lo tenéx en carcel,   con las cadenas también;
8 y las yaves de la carcel   consigo las tiene el reye.—
Ya meten las mezas puestas   y s'asentan al comer:
10 —Comeremos y beberemos,   a Don [Virgile] iremos a ver.—
Ya comieron y bebieron,   a Don Virgile fueron a ver:
12 —¿Qué hazéx, Don Virgile,   Don Virgile, qué hazéx?
—Peinando estó mis cabeyos   y la mi barbica también.

3*b*   *orig.* a rena mujere.

19

LAS HERMANAS REINA Y CAUTIVA (*i-a*)
(MP 48/H1)

Tetuán

   La mora Xarifa y mora,   la que mora en Almería,
2 dice que tiene deseo   de una cristiana cautiva.
   Los moros, como la oyeron,   de repente se partían;
4 de eyos iban para Francia,   de ellos para l'Almería.
   Y encuentraron al Conde Flores,   que a la marquesa traía;
6 libro de oro en la su mano,   las oraciones leía.
   Pidiendo iba al Dios del cielo   que le diera hijo o hija,
8 para heredarle los bienes,   que heredero no tenía.
   Ya matan al Conde Flores   y a la marquesa traían:
10 —Tómese, señora, la esclava,   ni es mora ni cristiana;
   tómese, señora, la esclava,   ni es hecha a la malicia.
12 —Tome, esclava, las yaves   de la dispensa y la cozina.
   —Yo las tomaré, señora,   por la gran desdicha suya;
14 ayer condesa de Flores,   hoy esclava en la cozina.—
   La reina estaba embarazada;   la esclava estaba lo mismo.
16 Van meses y vienen días,   las dos paren en un día.
   La reina pare una niña;   la esclava un niño tenía.
18 Las malas de las parteras,   por ganarse la platita,
   al niño daban a la reina;   la niña daban a la esclava.
20 Un día, lavando a la niña,   su madre bien la miraba.
   Con lágrimas de sus ojos,   la cara lava a la niña:
22 —¡O, hijita de mi alma!   ¡O, hijita de mi vida!
   Quién te me diera en la güerta,   la güerta de Andalucía!

24 Te nombrará Blanca Flor,   nombre de una hermana mía.
    La cautivaron los moros   día de Pascua Florida.—
26 Oyéndola está la reina,   onde su alto castío.
    Abajó por la escalera   como una leona brava:
28 —¿Qué señas tiene tu hermana?   ¿Qué señas eya tenía?
    —Lunar negro en el pecho,   siete vueltos le daría.—
30 Y de allí se conocieron   las dos hermanas cautivas.
    Otro día la mañana,   su libertad le daría.
32 —Dame al niño que mío   y toma el niño que tuyo.

---

32   *read* niña *in one case or the other*.

20

DON BUESO Y SU HERMANA (strophic)
(MP 49/H2)

20A. Salonika

   De las altas mares   traen a la niña;
2 cubierta la traen   de oro y perlería;
   en la su cabeza,   una piedra zafira;
4 más alelumbraba la noche   [que el] sol al mediodía.
   Los moricos malos   se la yevarían;
6 a la reina Izela   se la traerían.
   —¿Aquí qué me truxitex   a esta cautiva?
8 El rey es mancebo;   la toma por amiga.
   —Metelda, señora,   en esta cozina,
10 para que vos guize   unas ricas comidas.—
   Cuanto más la mete   en aqueya cozina,
12 más se la reciende   sus caras luzidas.
   —Metelda, señora,   a lavar al río.
14 Que piedra colores;   que cobra suspiros.—
   Cuanto más la mete   a lavar al río,
16 más se la reciende   su puerpo luzido.
   —Metelda, señora,   a lavar al vado.
18 Que piedra colores   y cobra aranco.—
   Más se la reciende   su cuerpo galano.
20 Inda no es de día,   ni amanecía,
   cuando la Blancaniña   lavaba y espandía.

18–19   *The verse*: Cuanto más la mete / a lavar al vado *should be supplied between vv.* 18 *and*
       19.

22 Su hermano don Bueso   por ayí pasaría:
  —¡O, qué manos blancas,   en el agua fría:
24 Enteras parecen   de una hermana mía.
  ¡O, qué manos blancas   en el agua yelada:
26 Enteras me parecen   a las de mi hermana.
  Dezidme, muchacha,   muchacha luzida,
28 si queréx venir   en la mi compaña.
  —Dezidme, muchacho,   muchacho luzido,
30 los paños del rey,   ¿ónde los dexaría?
  —Los que son de seda   al río los dexaríax.
32 Los que son de oro   consigo volos traeríax.—
  La subió al cabayo;   se la yevaría.
34 Por en medio del camino,   la niña hablaría:
  —Ya estamos cercana   a campos de Olivia.
36 —Dezidme, muchacha,   muchacha luzida,
  ¿de ónde vos sabíax   a campos de Oliva?
38 —Ayí fue criada,   ayí fue nacida.
  Como dexitex ende agora,   a mí me yevaría.
40 —Abridme vos, mi madre,   puertas del palacio.
  En lugar de nuera,   hija yo vos traigo.
42 —Si es mi nuera,   comande el mi palacio.
  Si es la mi heja,   en los mis brazos.

_____
28*b*   *read* compañía.

20*B*. Tetuán

  Lunes era, lunes,   de Pascua Florida.
2 Guerrean los moros   en los campos de Oliva.
  Ya la niña mora   yevan por cautiva.
4 Se la presentaran   a la reina mora:
  —Tome, señora,   esta prenda;
6 que en todo tu reino   no'y tan bonita.
  —Y el rey, que es pequeño,   la enamoraría.
8 —Mandéla, señora,   ya a lavar al río.
  Ayí dejaría   hermosura y brío.
10 Mandéla, señora,   con el pan al horno.
  Ayí dejaría   hermosura y rostro.—

12 Ya se iba la niña   con el pan al horno.
    Más se le acendía   hermosura y rostro.
14 Ya se iba la niña   a lavar al río.
    Más se la ardía   hermosura y brío.
16 Ente más tendía   y ente más lavaba.
    Un cabayero   por ayí venía:
18 —¡O, qué lindas manos   en el agua fría!
    ¡O, qué lindos pies   en el agua clara!
20 Si querís, señora,   vente en mi compaña.
    —De irme, señor,   de irme quería.
22 Paños de la reina   ¿a quén los dejaría?
    —Los de seda y grana,   traedlos contigo.
24 Los de lana y hilo,   tíralos al río.—
    Ya se iba la niña   con el cabayero.
26 ¿Por ónde pasaran?   Por los campos de Oliva.
    —Mi hermano don Güezo   y en eyos vendía.
28 Y en eyos vendía   oro y seda fina.
    —¿De ónde tú conoces   los campos de grana?
30 —Cuando yo chiquita   y en eyos vevía.
    —Abríme, mi madre,   puerta del palacio.
32 Por traervos nuera,   vuestra hija traigo.
    —Darte yo, mi hijo,   Seviya y Granada.
34 Darte yo, mi hijo,   los campos de grana.

33a,34a   Darte: *read* Darte he.

21

LA VUELTA DEL MARIDO (*í*)
(MP 58/I1)

Izmir

Arbolera, arbolera,   arbolera y tan gentil,
2 la raíz tiene de oro,   la simienta de marfil.
En la matica al alcabo,   hay una dama tan gentil.
4 —¿Qué buxcáx, la mi señora,   talas horas por aquí?
—Buxco yo al mi marido,   mi marido tan gentil.
6 —¿Qué me dax, la mi señora,   cual volo traigo aquí?
—Yo vos do mis tres molinos,   que me quedaron d'Amadí.
8 El uno mole cebada,   el otro mole jinjeví;
el más chiquitico de ellos,   harina baklavalí.
10 —¿Más qué me dax, mi señora,   cual volo traigo aquí?
—Yo vos do mis tres, mis hijas,   que quedaron d'Amadí.
12 La una para la meza,   la otra para servir;
la más chiquitica de eyas,   para roncar y dormir.
14 —¿Más qué me dax, mi señora,   cual volo traigo aquí?
—Más no tengo, cabayero,   para dar vos yo aquí.
16 —¿Me dax vuestro puerpo galano,   que quedó d'Amadí?
—Malaña tal cabayero,   que tal ayegó a dezir.
18 Se dieron a conocersen;   para caza ya se fueron.

22

LA VUELTA DEL MARIDO (é)
(MP 59/I2)

Tetuán

  —Soldadito, soldadito,   ¿si de la[s] guerras venid?
2 —Sí, señora, de la guerras,   de la guerras vengo yo.
  —¿Si has visto a su marido,   por fortuna alguna vez?
4 Su marido es alto y rubio   y alto como un elflé.
  Y yeva la media de seda,   zapatito de babé.
6 —Ese hombre, que Vd. dice,   muerto está más de un mes.
  Y en su testamento deja   que me caze con Vd.
8 —No permita Dios del cielo,   ni lo quiera yo también.
  Siete años m'he esperado   y otros siete esperaré.
10 Si a los siete no viene,   monja yo me quedaré;
  monja yo de Santa Clara,   monja yo de Santa Inglé.
12 Tres hijitas, que yo tengo,   yo les acomodaré;
  la una con doña Juana,   la otra con doña Inglé;
14 y la chiquitica de eyas   conmigo la dejaré;
  que me peine y que me lave,   que me traiga de comer.
16 —Déme un jarro de agua,   que yego muerto de sed.
  —Ni tengo jarro, ni jarra,   donde darte a beber.
18 —Démelo en tu boquita,   que es más dulce que la miel.—
  Vueltas dieron al palacio   por podersen conocer.
20 Y de ayí se conocieron   el marido y la mujer.
  Hízole cama de rosa,   cabecera de azojar;
22 cobertón con que se tape,   con hojas de un limonar.

23

EL CONDE NIÑO (*á*)
(MP 55/J1)

23*A*. Salonika

En el vergel de la reina, hay crecido un bel rozal.
2 La raíz tiene de oro y la cimiente de un bel cristal.
En la ramica más alta, un ruxibón sentí cantar.
4 El cantar que va diziendo, gloria es de lo escuchar.
La reina estaba labrando y la hija durmiendo está.
6 —Alevantéx, la mi hija, del vuestro dulce folgar.
Venid, veréx como canta la serenica de la mar.
8 —No es serena, mi madre, sino es el conde Alimar,
que con mí quijo reíre y que con mí quijo burlar.
10 —Si es esto, la mi hija, yo lo mandaré matar.
—No lo matéx, la mi madre, ni lo quijerex matar.
12 El conde es niño y muchacho, el mundo quiere gozar.
Desterrarldo de estas tierras, de aquí no coma pan.—
14 La reina, que de mal tenga, presto los manda a matar.
Matólos y degoyólos y los mandó a enterrar.
16 El se hizo una graviyina; eya se hizo una conjá.
La reina, desde que lo supo, presto los mandó arancar.
18 Arancólos y deshojólos y los mandó echar a volar.
Eya se hizo un[a] paloma y él se hizo un gavilán.
20 La reina, desde que lo supo, presto los mandó aferrar.
Aferrólos y degoyólos y los mandó echar a la mar.
22 Eya se hizo una perquia y él se hizo una cara sazán.
La reina, desde que lo supo, presto los mandó a pexcar.

46

24 Pexcólos y degoyólos   y los metió a cozinar.
   Al fin de la mediodía,   los quitó por almorzar.
26 Las espinas que salieron,   las enterró en su portal.
   Eya se hizo una culebra   y él se hizo un alacrán.
28 En el cueyo de la reina,   se le hue asarrear.

23*B*. Tangier

Levantóse el conde Niño,   mañanita de San Juan.
2 Fue a darle agua a su cabayo,   a la oriya de la mar.
   Mientras los cabayos beben,   el conde dice un cantar.
4 Mujeres, que están encinta,   las hacía abultar.
   Güertas, que están cerradas,   se abran de par en par.
6 —Si oís, la niña infanta,   si durméis o despertáis,
   si oís como canta   la serena de la mar.
8 —No es la serena, mi madre,   ni menos lo su cantar;
   el conde Niño, mi madre,   que a mí viene a demandar.
10 —Si a ti demanda, la infanta,   yo le mandaré a matar.
   —Si lo matareis, mi madre,   juntos nos han de enterrar.—
12 La reina, con tanta rabia,   los mandara a matar.
   De eya corrió leche y sangre   y de él corriera sangre real.
14 Muere el uno y muere el otro;   ya los mandan a enterrar.
   De eya salió una toronja   y de él creciera un limonar.
16 Crece el uno y crece el otro,   los dos se van a juntar.
   La reina, con grande celo,   los mandare a cortar.
18 De eya sale una paloma   y de él saliera un gavilán.
   Vola uno, vola otro,   y al cielo van a juzgar.

5*a* Güertas: *read* Cuertas ('doors').
8*b* lo su [*sic*].

24

DIEGO LEÓN (*á-a*)
(MP 63/J5)

Tangier

   Y en la ciudad de Toledo   y en la ciudad de Granada,
2 ayí se criaba un mancebo,   que por nombre León se yamaba.
   Y él era alto de cuerpo,   morenito de su cara,
4 delgadito de cintura,   mozo criado entre damas.
   De una tal s'enamoró,   de una muy rica yamada.
6 Se miran por una reja,   también por una ventana.
   Y el día que no se ven   no les aprovecha nada.
8 Ni les aprovecha el pan,   ni la agua de la mañana,
   ni les aprovecha el dinero   con que León negociaba.
10 Un día se vieron juntos,   la dize:—Bien de mi alma,
   mañana te hay de pedir;   no sé si es coza cercana.—
12 Lo que la dama arresponde,   lo que a León agradaba.
   Y otro día por la mañana,   con don Pedro se encontrara.
14 De rodiyas en el suelo,   los buenos días le daba:
   —Don Pedro, dame a tu hija   y a tu hija doña Juana.
16 —Mi hija no es de casar,   porque aún [es] chica y muchacha.—
   Por hacer burla del caso,   ya a su hija le contara:
18 —Hija, León te ha pedido;   váyase en hora mala.
   El [que] mi yerno ha de ser   ha de menester que traiga
20 de caudal con mil ducados   y otros de oro y plata
   y otros tantos te daré,   hija querida de mi alma.
22 —Padre, cásame con él   y aunque me deis nada.
   Que los bienes de este mundo   ya los daba y los yevaba.—

24 Y él la cerró en un aposento,   porque con León no hablara.
    Alquiló cuatro valientes,   los mejores de la plaza,
26 que mataran a León   y le quitaran el alma.
    León ya los tres mató   y el uno herido estaba.
28 Unos dizen que murió   y otros dizen le vieron;
    y otros dizen que le vieron   al otra parte de la agua.
30 No son tres días pasados,   León en la plaza estaba.
    Alzó tres chinas del suelo,   ronjólas a la ventana:
32 —Mi dama que no arresponde,   es seña que está trocada.
    —No estoy trocada, León,   que aún estoy en mi palabra.—
34 Y otro día en la mañana,   ricas bodas s'armaban.
    El novio yeva la novia   y la gente la noche mala.

25

LA AMANTE ABANDONADA (polyas.)
(K2)

Salonika

Un amor tan querensiozo, que olvidar no lo podía;
2 la mañanica y la tarde, a vijitar la verría.
Si la toparía durmiendo, la cubijaba y se ía.
4 Si la toparía despierta, a platicar se metía:
—¿De qué yoráx, cativada? ¿De qué yoráx? ¿Qué tem[í]ax?
6 O estáx recién preñada, o teníax mal de amores.
—Ni tenía de amores, ni estó recién preñada.
8 Si volo conto, el buen reye, ¿afearéx mis palabras?
—Yo ḥue criada en Seviya y entre buena gente honrada.
10 Un cabayero, Andarleto, que de mí se namorara,
tres noches durmió con eya, le pareció tres semanas.—
12 Escalera de oro le hizo, debaxo de sus ventanas,
para que suba y abaxe, como si fuera su caza.
14 Y en fin de las tres noches, se fue a buxcar nueva amada.

7a *read* Ni tenía [mal] de amores.

26

EL PÁJARO VERDE (*á-a*)
(MP 66/K5)

Tangier

Por la caye de Madrid,   se cría una hermosa dama.
2 Esa tal no tiene padre,   pero poco le faltaba,
con un padrasto que tenía,   más que a su hija l'amaba.
4 No la casan porque es joven,   porque un pariente le guarda.
Y en frente de eya vivía   un joven de buena cara.
6 Tanto se quieren los dos,   que con la vista se hablan.
También se hablan a solas,   por una baja ventana.
8 Un día la dice el joven,   la dice:—Bien de mi alma,
una pena tengo en mi pecho;   contar te quiero la causa.
10 Que tu tío t'ha pedido,   hombre de gran importancia.
—No esté de nada, mi vida,   no esté de nada, mi alma.
12 Basta que tú seas hombre   para seguir tu palabra.
Yo también seré mujer,   para salir de mi casa.
14 Con lo poco que tú tengas   y lo mucho que yo traiga;
las haciendas de mi padre   para mí no son negadas.—
16 El joven se fue contento   y la dama s'entró gustosa.
Ya se[r]ía la mañanita,   su madre la despertaba:
18 —Levanta, hija, la dice,   levanta, hija en el alma.
Te casarás con tu tío,   hombre de gran importancia.
20 —Déjeme, madre, durmiendo,   que más bien estoy en mi cama.—
De ayí la reconoce   que de amor está tocada.

---

11 No esté de nada: *read* No se te dé nada.

51

22 Ya baja las escaleras   como una leona brava.
    Que de primos y parientes   armará una gran escuadra.
24 Seguiéronse para el campo   donde el joven trabajaba.
    Lo pían desimulado;   le pegan tres puñaladas.
26 Yega la nueva a la dama;   la dama no se creía,
    hasta que oye tocar   sentimiento de campana.
28 De sus cabeyos se tira,   de sus cabeyos s'arrastra.
    Fuérase hasta su tía,   hasta su tía l'amada.
30 Su tía la va diciendo: . . . .
    —Si el joven se murió,   Dios le perdone su alma.
32 Te casarás con tu tío,   hombre de gran importancia.
    —Yo no salgo de este cuarto,   si no salgo amortajada.—
34 Sangre de su pecho izquierdo,   sangre de su pecho izquierdo.
    Juntos se enterraron los dos   y juntitos en un prado.
36 De eya sale una azucena   y de él sale un clavel blanco.

27

EL CONDE ALARCOS (*í-a*)
(MP 64/L1)

Salonika

   Triste iba la enfalta,   triste más de cada día,
2 porque no la cazó el padre,   ni en su cuidado tenía.
   Mosas, qu'eran de quince años,   marido e hijos tenían.
4 Eya, que es de veinticuatro,   por e[s]pozar la tenía:
   —Vuestra culpa es, la infalta,   vuestra, que no era la mía.
6 Vos ya estuvierex cazada   con el conde de Seviya.
   Agora ya está cazado,   mujer y hijos tenía.

28

LA MALA SUEGRA (*á-e*)
(MP 70/L4)

28*A*. Salonika

. . . Así lo sentiré dizire y de buena gente contare:
2 Los bienes de este mundo, como vienen así se vayen.
La suegra con la nuera siempre se quijeron male.
4 El esfuegro con el yerno, como el sol de invierno,
que sale tarde y se cerra presto.
6 La hija con la madre, como la uña en la carne.
El padre con el hijo, como la piedra en el aniyo.

28*B*. Çanakkale (Dardanelles)

Dolores tiene la reina, no los puede soportar.
2 —¡Quén estuviera en el saray de mi padre,
para tenerla por vezina a la condesa la mi madre!
4 Cuando me toman las dolores, que me tenga piadades.
—Vate tú, la mi elmuera, a parir ande tu madre,
6 . . . . que te tenga piadades.
Si es por tu marido, gayinas le do almorzare.
8 Si es por el mi hijo, pichones le do al cenares.—
S'alevanta l'almuera, con contentés de la su eshuegra.
10 Se va a parir ande su padre; a la tadre viene su marido:
—A todos veo en medio; a la mi esposa no veo.
12 —¿Qué te diré, mi hijo? Se fue a parir ande su padre.
A mí me dixo puta vieja; a ti, hijo de mal padre.—

54

14 Con saña grande,   tomó espada en su mano.
   Y fue para matarla;   ya baxa la su madre,
16 para recibir a su yerno   con gusto y alegría:
   —En buen simán mos sea el hijo,   que se críe con padre y madre.
18 —¡Mal simán sea el hijo,   que arevente con la madre!
   —¿Qué hablas hablas, mi hijo,   o mi hijo de mi cara?
20 —Porque a mi madre le dixo puta vieja   y a mí, hijo de mal padre.
   —Si lo dixo la mi hija,   de la cama que no s'alevante.
22 Si es malmetido de eya,   con ayuda del Dio, gota grande que le
   caiga.—
   Estas palabras diziendo,   la reina caía y se moría.
24 Cara haberes que vaya al rey,   que la madre se le moría.
   En esto se creyó él   que era malmetido de eya.
26 El buen simán que nos sea el hijo,   que se lo cría con sus pechos.

29

LA MALCASADA DEL PASTOR (ó) +
JUAN LORENZO (á)
(MP 72/L8 + MP 12/C2)

Tetuán (or **Tangier**?)

   —Cazárome mi padre   con un pastor,
2 que en toda la pastoría   no le hubo mejor.
   El me mata y me quiere   la sinrazón.—
4 Con cantarito de agua,   antes que amanezca el sol;
   ya ía la media noche;   el sueño la venció.
6 Y vio que la tocaba un cabayero   que a eya la bezó.
   —Tate, tate, el cabayero,   cazado yo.
8 Si mi marido lo sabe,   quitada seré yo.
   —Tú sos mi linda mujer   y yo su lindo marido.—
10 Y en palmas de sus manos   a su caza la yevó.
   —Y ahora sé que soy   tu honrada mujer yo.—
12 —Vide venir un navío   sobre aguas de la mar.
   Las tablas de aquel navío   eran de un fino coral;
14 las velas de aquel navío   eran de un fino arexclat;
   las cuerdas de aquel navío   eran de oro torsar.—
16 Dentro viene Juan Lorenzo;   ir al rey viene a convidar;
   ya gaínas, ya pichones,   palomas de un palomar;
18 vino tinto, vino claro,   lo mejor de Portugal.
   Y en meatad de aquel almuerzo,   mandó el rey a pregonar:

1a *read* Cazáronme mis padres *or* Cazárame mi padre.
7b *read* casada.

20 —Quien tiene mujer hermoza   que la saque a pasear.—
La mujer de Juan Lorenzo   sola sale a pasear.
22 Fuese el rey de güerta en güerta   y de roza en el rozal.
Y escogió el rey una roza   del mejor de su rozal:
24 —Tome, señora, esta roza,   la mejor de mi rozal.
Que entre todas las hermozas,   no he visto tu par igual.—
26 El rey, como era pequeño,   su halda s'echó a espulgar.
—Mataremos a Juan Lorenzo;   me pondré yo en su lugar.—
28 —No hagáis tal, mi señore,   ni se os ponga en voluntad.
Mandaile de güerta en güerta   y de civdad en civdad.—
30 Sacó una navajita aguda   y degoyarle por detrás.

26*b* *read* en su halda.

30

LA MUJER ENGAÑADA (*í-a*)
(MP 74/L13)

Izmir

    —Dúrmete, mi alma,   dúrmite, mi vista,
2 que tu padre viene   d'onde nueva amiga.
    —Abriméx, mi alma,   abriméx, mi vista.
4 Que vengo cansado   de arar las viñas.
    —Ni veníx cansado,   ni veníx manido,
6 sino que veníx   d'onde nueva amiga.
    Entrí más adientro,   por ver lo que havía:
8 Vide mezas puestas,   con ricas comidas;
    salero de oro,   sal de Melajía,
10 cuchiyo de plata,   pechita d'holanda.
    Entrí más adientro,   por ver lo que había:
12 Vide camas armadas,   con ricas cortinas;
    eya con camizica   y él con extunico;
14 la cara encalada,   la ceja enteñida.
    Ni es más hermoza,   ni es más valida,
16 ni yeva las joyas,   las que yo vestía.

31

EL RAPTO (í-a)
(MP 94/O5)

Tangier

  Una blanca niña,   que en todas mis gansas
2 no hubo tan linda   como Blancaniña.
  —Vuestras manos blancas   son preziones mías.
4 Matáis a los hombres   que van por la vía.
  —Vate con Dios, conde,   mira que soy niña.
6 Si mi padre lo sabe,   por Dios, Catuliña.
  Yo no entrato amores,   sólo almohadita;
8 en eyas labraba   y en eyos cosía;
  en eyas gastaba   oro y seda fina.—
10 Ya alzóla en sus brazos   y a la mar la vola:
  Yoros y bramidos   de Blancaniña.
12 —No yoréis, mi vida,   no yoréis, mi alma.
  No reguís por campo   estas perlas finas.
14 Ni vos yevo hurtado,   ni menos cautiva.
  Vos yevo a ser reina   de la Andalucía.
16 Sacaré a tu madre   de la cozinería.
  La pondré yo reina   de las tierras mías.
18 Sacaré a tu padre   de la pescadería.
  Le pondré alcalde   de las tierras mías.
20 Sacaré a tu hermano   de la morería.
  Le pondré alcalde   de las haciendas mías.—
22 Otro día en la mañana,   ricas bodas s'armaría.

7a *read* Yo no trato en amores.
7b *read* almohaditas.
10a *orig.* su brazos
14a *read* hurtada.

32

EL FORZADOR (*í-a*)
(MP 96/O7)

Salonika

> En mis güertas crecen flores   y en los sacsís gravinas.
> 2 Por ayí pasó un cabayero   cargado de oro y perlería.
> S'aparan damas y donzeyas   por tala maraviya.
> 4 Del relumbrador de las donzeyas,   el cabayo ya no le camina.
> Echó los ojos en alto;   s'enamoró de la más chica.
> 6 Le prometió todos sus bienes,   por ver si en él quería.
> —Más muchos tiene el mi padre,   que un conde de Sevía.—
> 8 El cabayero, que es mancebo,   sus mientes ayí metía.
> Caminos de quinze días   en siete ya lo haría.
> 10 A la fin de la media noche,   a la puerta le batería.
> Topó la puerta cerrada   y ventanas que no se abrían.
> 12 Con palabras de encantamiento,   d'en par en par las abriría.
> Metióle puño en sus pechos,   por ver si se consentía.
> 14 Despertóse la donzeya,   con gran temblor y manzía:
> —Vate, vate, cabayero,   vate, vate, por tu vía.
> 16 Si de aquí te echo un grito,   te acojo todo Sevía.

6*b* en: *read* an.

33

SILVANA (*í-a*)
(MP 98/P1)

Salonika

Se pasea la Silvana   por un corral que tenía,
2 virgüela de oro en su mano   y muy bien la tañía.
    Mejor tañe y mejor tembla   y mejor romanzas dezía.
4 De ayí la oyó su padre,   d'altas torres d'ayí arriba:
    —Esta boz, que aquí siento,   de Silvana me parecía.
6 Subiréx aquí, Silvana,   suberéx, la hija mía.
    Muy bien pareséx, Silvana,   con sayos de seda fina,
8 más que la reina, la vuestra madre,   cuando de oro vestía.
    ¿Si vos plazía, Silvana,   de ser amiga mía?
10 —Plazer me dize, mi padre,   plazer y descortesía.
    Déxeme ir a los baños,   a los baños de agua fría,
12 a lavarme y entrenzarme   y mudarme una camisa,
    como uzaba mi madre,   cuando con el rey durmía.—
14 Ya se partía Silvana,   ya se parte y se ía.
    De los sus ojos yoraba   y de la su boca dezía:
16 —¡Oíme, el Dio del cielo,   y también la madre mía!—
    De ayí la oyó la madre,   de altas torres de arriba.
18 —Esta boz, que la que siento,   de Silvana me parecía.
    Suberéx aquí, Silvana,   suberéx aquí arriba.
20 Contaréx vuestros enojos   y la vuestra melancolía.
    —¿Qué le contaré, mi madre,   que vergüenza me parecía:
22 Un padre, que a mí ha criado,   de amore me acometería.
    —Para la muerte no hay remedio;   para la vida mucho había.—

24 Pregón echara la reina,   que no aciendan candelería.
  —Troquemos nuestros vestidos;   los vuestros yo metería.—
26 Ya s'esparte la reina,   para ande el buen rey ía.
  Al fin de la media noche,   la honra le demandaría.
28 —Madre que parió a Silvana,   ¿qué honra le quedaría?
  —¡O, qué hija buena tengo,   que de pecado me quetaría!

34

DELGADINA (*á-a*)
(MP 99/P2)

Salonika

Tres hijas tiene el buen reye, todas las tres como la carta.
2 La una se yama Oro y la otra Plata se yama;
la chiquita de eyas Delgadina se yamaba.
4 Un día, estando en la misa, el su padre l'hay mirado.
—¿Qué me mira, el mi padre, qué me mira y qué me ama?
6 —Te miro yo, Delgadina, que has de ser m'enamorada.
—No lo quere el Dio del cielo, ni mi madre la honrada,
8 ser comlesa de mi madre y madrasta de mi hermana.

35

GERINELDO (*í-o*)
(MP 101/Q1)

Tangier

Quién tuviera tal fortuna   para ganar lo perdido,
2   como tuvo Gerineldo   mañanita de domingo,
cortando paños de seda   para dar al rey vestidos.
4   Mirándole está la reina   desde su alto castío:
—Girineldo, Girineldo,   mi cabayero pulido,
6   ¡quién te me diera esta noche   tres horas en mi servicio!
—Como soy vuestro criado,   señora, burláis conmigo.
8   —Yo no burlo, Girineldo,   que de verás te lo digo.
—¿A qué horas vendré, señora,   y a qué horas daré al castío?
10   —A horas de la medianoche,   cuando el rey está vencido;
cuando canta el primer gayo   . . . .
12   Estas horas son las doce,   cuando el rey está durmido;
con zapatitos de seda,   para que no hagáis ruido.—
14   Medianoche es pasada;   Girineldo no ha venido.
Eya en estas palabras,   Girineldo dio sospiro.
16   —¿Quién es este atrevido   que suspira en mi castío?
—Girineldo soy, señora,   que vengo a lo prometido.
18   —Malhaya tú, Girineldo,   quien amor puzo contigo.
Medianoche ya es pasada   y tú no habéis venido.—
20   Púzole escalera de oro;   por eya subió el castío.
Que de besos y abrasos,   de sueño los ha vencido.
22   Eyos en el dulce sueño   y el buen rey ha consentido.
Miró escalera de oro;   por eya se subió al castío.

20*a*,23*a*   oro: *orig.* ora.

24 Y encontró a Girineldo   como mujer y marido:
  —¿Qué haré de mis mezquinos?   [¿Qué haré de mis mezquinos?]
26 Si yo mato a Girineldo,   mi reino será perdido.
  Si yo mato a la reina,   viveré con su suspiro.
28 Más vale que yo me caye   y no se lo diga a ninguno,
  como la mujer que tapa   las faltas de su marido.—
30 Sacó espada de su cinto;   se la puso por testigo.
  —Levantéis, Girineldo,   que los dos vamos perdidos.
32 Que la espada de mi padre   ya tenemos por testigo.—
  Ya se sale Girineldo   tan triste y tan dolerido.
34 Por encuentro encuentra al rey   saliendo de su castío:
  —¿Dónde vienes, Girineldo,   tan triste y tan amariyo?
36 —Del jardín vengo, el señore,   de cortar rozas y lirios.
  La fragrancia de una rosa   m'ha trastornado el sentido.
38 —Mientes, mientes, Girineldo,   con la princés has durmido.
  —Matéisme, mi señor rey,   que la culpa ya ha tenido.
40 —No te mato, Girineldo,   serás mi querido yerno.
  —Juramento tengo hecho   en mi librito vize'ro [. . .].

25b   *Repetition of the hemistich is indicated by the word* bis *in the original.*
38b   princés: *read* princesa.
39b   ya ha: *read* yo he.

36

REPULSA Y COMPASIÓN (*á*)
(MP 115/S5)

Tetuán

    —Yo me levantara un lunes,   un lunes antes del sol.
2 Tomé cantarita en mano   y a la mar le fui henchir.
    A meatad de aquel camino,   con un paje me encontrí.
4 Tocóme la mano al pecho,   que de mí quizo burlar.
    Y le di un entrepecho,   que a la mar le fui echar.—
6 Y después que le tirara,   ya se asentaba a yorar:
    —Duele mi corazón, duele,   de verle así ahogar.—
8 Y tirara a mi trenzado,   por poderle yo escapar.

1*b*   *orig.* antel.

37

EL SUEÑO DE LA HIJA (polyas.)
(MP 68, 129/S6)

Izmir

El rey de Francia   tres hijas tenía;
2 la una labraba,   la otra cozía;
la chica de eyas   bastidor hazía.
4 Labrando, labrando,   esfueño le caía.
La madre la vido,   aharvar la iba.
6 —No me aharvéx, madre,   ni m'aharvaríax.
Esfueño me soñaba   de bien y alegría.
8 M'aparí al pozo,   vide un pilar de oro,
con tres paxaricos   picando el oro.
10 M'aparí a la ventana,   vide una estreya diana.
M'aparí a la puerta,   vide la luna entera.
12 —El pilar de oro,   hijo del rey tu novio.
Los tres paxaricos   son tres cuñadicos;
14 la'streya diana,   la reina tu cuñada
y la luna entera,   la reina tu esfuegra.

38

EL POZO AIRÓN (ó)
(X13)

Salonika

Ya se van los siete hermanos,   ya se van para Aragón.
2 Las calores eran fuertes;   agua no se les topó.
Por el medio del camino,   toparon un pojo airón.
4 Echaron pares y nones,   al más chico le cayó.
Ya lo atan con la cuerda,   lo echan al pojo airón.
6 Por el medio del pojo,   la cuerda se le rompió.
El agua se le hizo sangre   y las piedras culebras son;
8 culebras y alacranes   que le comen el corasón.
Ya se van los seis hermanos,   amargos de corasón.
10 —Si vos pregunta la mi madre,   le diréx atrás quedó.
Si vos pregunta el mi padre,   le dizíx al pojo airón.
12 Si vos preguntan los mis hijos,   le diréx güérfanos son.
Si vos pregunta mi mujer,   bivda quedó.

39

LA SIERPE DEL RÍO (*í-o*)
(X15)

Salonika

    Allí en Antequera   había un molino.
2 No muele con agua,   ni muele con vino,
    sino con la sangre   de los cristianicos;
4 sino con la sangre   de los Galanzanos.
    Enfrente había   un rico palacio;
6 adientro había   un rico castiyo.
    Abrevando estaban   al beber del vino.
8 Le habló el tío,   también el sobrino,
    que le dé a la sierpe,   a la sierpe del río.
10 De la prima alba, cuando alborea,   ya le da la hija,
    de la prima noche   fin el gayo del día.
12 —Dexedes, mi tío,   de ir en aquel castiyo.
    Entraréx, mi tío,   en aquel palacio.
14 Ayí hay doje reyes   de oro encoronados.
    Eyos vos dan cuchiyos;   eyos vos dan cabayos.

10*a* *orig.* albroea.

NOTES AND
ENGLISH ABSTRACTS

1. *El destierro del Cid (á-o)* + *Las quejas de Jimena (á-e)* (*The Banishment of the Cid + Jimena's Complaint*) (MP 5/A9 + MP 3/A3) (**Tetuán**): The king asks the Cid (el Cidi) where he has been. His beard is long and his hair has become curly and grey. The king has heard that he has conquered "towns and castles." He answers that he has been fighting the Moors. The king suggests that he share his booty with Count Ordóñez (Ordoño; Adoña; Alarcos; Niño). The Cid refuses to give him anything; his victories have cost him dearly and the blood of many nobles has been shed. The king orders the Cid arrested. No one dares touch him except Count Ordóñez. The Cid chops the count's head off and throws it at the king's feet. He reproaches the Cid and orders him exiled for a year. The Cid answers that he will go for four years and considers himself dishonored to be the king's vassal. He scorns the lands and tents of the king; those of his father are worth more. The Cid rides off into exile, but the king orders his knights to make him return, so that such a brave man will not leave his kingdom.

Our text only includes fragments of *El destierro del Cid*: the initial dialogue, with the king's order to share what he has conquered with Count Ordóñez (vv. 1–5), and the Cid's arrogant reply that he will go into exile of his own free will (8–9). V. 9, which is formulistic, usually comes after v. 7, but here serves as a rather effective bridge between two unrelated scenes by juxtaposing Count Ordóñez's death with that of Jimena's father (v. 11), thus creating a cohesive narrative that is not altogether unlike that of the *Mocedades de Rodrigo*, from which, of course, derive not only *Las quejas de Jimena* but also the interpolated verses, "Por besar tu mano, Reye . . ." (Bénichou, *Creación*, p. 16), present in some versions of *El destierro*. The contamination *Destierro + Quejas* is abundantly documented (CMP A9.3, 6, 10–11; A3.2–3, 7; Librowicz 1).

Bibliography: Luria MS 1.
/ Arce 2; ASK 5(2); Bennaim MS 37; CMP 9.1–11; FRS 5; Larrea 6–7; Larrea, "Romances hispánicos," p. 53 (= Larrea 7); Librowicz 1; Librowicz (II) A6; MP 5 (= CMP A9.1); PTJ 6–6a (= Sánchez Moguel); Sánchez Moguel 1–2.

73

//Catalán, "Memoria," p. 458.

///Catalán ("Memoria," pp. 457−461) has discovered a seventeenth-century Peninsular version: "¿De dónde venís, el Cid,/que en cortes no abéis estado?" Bénichou's exhaustive study (*Creación*, pp. 13−39) is fundamentally important.

Vv. 10−18 constitute a reasonably "complete" version of *Las quejas de Jimena:* Ximena appears before King León one afternoon to ask for justice in the matter of her father's death. She complains that each day she must see the person who killed her father. It is the Cid, who feeds his falcon on the doves in her dovecote. She reproaches the king and he decides to marry her to the Cid. And so Ximena happily leaves the palace, thanking God for her good fortune, and is married to the man who killed her father.

Bibliography:

/Alvar, *Textos*, II, 773 (= Bénichou); Arce 3; ASK 3(5); Bénichou 32; Bennaim MS 37; Boas−Nahón 1; CMP A3.1−8; FRS 2; Larrea 2−3; Librowicz 1; Librowicz(II) A3; MP 3(= CMP A3.1); MRuiz 37A.5−9; Nahón 1A−1B; PTJ 3−3a (3 = Bénichou); Pulido, p. 54 (= MP); Yurchenco, p. 131.

//Braga, II, 249.

///*Primav.* 30, 30a-b; Durán 735 (Cada día que amanece/veo quien mató a mi padre; En Burgos está el buen rey/asentado a su yantar; Día era de los Reyes,/día era señalado; Delante el rey de León/doña Jimena una tarde). See Paul Bénichou, "El casamiento del Cid," *NRFH*, 7 (1953), 316−336, and "Sobre el casamiento del Cid," *NRFH*, 8 (1954), 79; also Bénichou, pp. 32−34, and Nahón 1.

2. *Almerique de Narbona (í)* + *Roncesvalles (í)* + *Las bodas en París (í)* (*Aymeri of Narbonne* + *The Battle of Roncevaux* + *The Wedding Feast in Paris*) (MP 20/B8 + MP 20/B3 + MP 95/M14): (**Salonika**): Vv. 1−3 pertain to *Almerique:* The count fits out a great fleet, launches it on the [river] San Gil (*sangír*), and sets out for France.

Bibliography: ASK 20(2); Attias 32; CMP B8; Coello 8; FRS 7; Gil 25 (= Coello); Hemsi 14; idem, "Evocation," pp. 1056a, 1091 (= Hemsi 14); Hollander 1; MP 20 (= Coello); PTJ 20 (= Attias); UYA 263 (= GSA = *Yoná* 2A); *Yoná* 2A−2B.

///*Primav.* 196 (Del Soldán de Babilonia, /de ése os quiero decir). See our study in *Yoná* 2 (pp. 60−62, 66).

Vv. 4−8 represent *Roncesvalles*: [Roldán] urges the French to return to battle. If the grand duke (great count, great Frenchman) learns they have fled, he will deny them bread and traveling money and will prohibit them from sleeping with [their] ladies. In their counterattack, they kill seventy thousand of the enemy and countless footsoldiers.

Bibliography: Identical to *Almerique*, but see also TCR C2.

///*Primav.* 183; ASW 67, 127 (Domingo era de Ramos,/la Pasión quieren decir; Ya comienzan los franceses/con los moros pelear). See *Yoná*, pp. 62, 66.

Vv. 9−23 are an extensive fragment of *Las bodas en París*, but the colorful initial scene of the dancing *damas* and *caballeros* and the count propositioning the lady who leads the dance has been forgotten: There is a great wedding feast in France, in the halls of Paris (Marfil). The king's son is marrying Amadí's (Almaví's or the vizier's) daughter. More than a thousand knights and ladies are dancing. The count (Amadí, etc.) is watching a fine lady who is leading the dance. She asks him why he is looking at her and, if he is attracted to her, suggests he take her along with him. Her husband has gone on a trip (or has gone to war; is far away) and the other members of her family will not notice her departure. The count wraps her in a golden cloak and carries her off, leaving one slipper exposed. As he goes downstairs, one of her slippers falls off. As he goes out the door (along the way), he meets her husband (Amadí(n), Almadí, Almaví). He asks the count what he is carrying and the count answers that it's a little page (a little golden bird), who has become sick (which he has just caught; just bought; used to serve him). The husband recognizes the slipper, which he has just bought. The count starts to flee, but the husband says he should not run away; he himself is to blame for having neglected his beautiful wife.

Bibliography: ASK 20(2); Attias 32.24−77; CMP M14.1−14; Coello 8.9−30; FRS 7; Gil 25 (= Coello); Hemsi 14.9−31; idem, "Evocation," pp. 1056*a*, 1091 (= Hemsi 14); Hollander 1.6−7; PTJ 95 (= Attias); UYA 263−265 (vv. 10 ff.; = GSA = *Yoná* 2A); *Yoná* 2A.10−33, 2*B*.1−22.

/Alvar, *Textos*, II, 760 (vv. 24−45); ASK 95(8); Bénichou 138; CMP M14.15−22; Larrea 142−143; Librowicz (II) M14; Librowicz, "Gibraltar," no. 10; MP 95; MRuiz 78*A-C*; Nahón 38; Ortega 214; PTJ 95*a* (= Alvar, *Textos*).

//VRP 416.

///*Primav.* 157; ASW 123, 144 (Bodas hacían en Francia/allá dentro en París; Bodas se hazen en Francia/allá dentro en París).

3. *El sueño de doña Alda* (*á-e*) + *Melisenda insomne* (*á-e*) (*Lady Alda's Dream* + *Sleepless Melisenda*) (MP 21/B6 + MP 28/B17) (**Salonika**): Vv. 1*a*, 2, 3*b*, 4−5, 14, 16−18 pertain to *El sueño de doña Alda*. V. 1*b* is taken from *Melisenda sale de los baños*; v. 3*a* from the fragment of *El moro de Antequera* which serves as a prologue to Salonikan forms of *El conde Alemán y la reina*. See Attias 13.10 and Yoná 7A.4. The Eastern Sephardic narrative of *El sueño de doña Alda* can be summarized as follows: Alda, Roland's (Rovdale) betrothed, is in Paris, surrounded by her three hundred handmaidens. Two hundred (or all) are spinning and doing embroidery (grinding gold) and one hundred are playing musical instruments. Alda falls asleep. She sleeps for three days and three nights and awakes in terror. She orders her ladies to interpret her dream: She has seen a heron flying over the fields of Alsume [accompanied by a falcon?]. According to an aged crone [from *Melisenda insomne*], the birds represent Alda and her beloved, the count.

Benardete's version is remarkable in that it is the only Eastern text we have seen that preserves a vestige of what seems to be the dream's original bird imagery. Compare also Menéndez Pidal, "El Romancero y los sefardíes," p. xxii, though we suspect this text is synthetic. Other Eastern versions have taken over another ominous bird dream from *El nacimiento de Montesinos* (*á-e*) (Attias 28.29−32; CMP B6.3−4; *Yoná* 3.15−16).

Bibliography: Attias 28; CMP B6.1−4; FRS 8A (= *Yoná*); Menéndez Pidal, "El Romancero y los sefardíes," p. xxii; RoH, I, 401; SRC PB3; *Yoná* 3.

/Alvar, *Textos*, II, 763; ASK 21(4); Bénichou 57; Bennaim MS 76; Cantera Burgos, pp. 12−13; CMP B6.5−17; Fereres MS 23; FRS 8*B*; Gil 51 (= MP); Larrea 24−25, 65.27−66; Librowicz (II) B6; Menéndez Pidal, "El romancero sefardí: Su extraordinario carácter," p. 557; MP 21 (= CMP B6.5); MRuiz 34; PTJ 21−21*a* (= Alvar, *Textos*; MRuiz).

///*Primav*. 184 (En París está doña Alda,/la esposa de don Roldán). Note also the Eastern *incipit* dated in 1628 and 1753, "En París está [Doñalda]" and also "Un sueño soñí [mis dueñas]" (1594 and 1599) (Avenary, "Cantos," nos. 73 and 195). For studies on *El sueño de doña Alda* and further bibliography, see Bénichou 57−59; Nahón 4; Yoná 3.

The contamination of *El sueño de doña Alda* and *Melisenda insomne*, which is traditional in Salonika and Larissa, undoubtedly takes place because of the near identity of the protagonists' consultations with their ladies-in-waiting (cf.

Attias 33.21−28; CMP B6.3; B17.10, 13; SRC PB3). Benardete's and other Salonikan texts (Attias; SRC) are remarkable in preserving the name of Melisenda's beloved. Most Eastern texts are radically reduced to a dialogue between three sisters and the admonition to enjoy youth while it lasts (*Bosnia* C1). The extended description of the heroine's finery (vv. 19−25) is extraneous here, though it was probably initially suggested by the words "l'ajugar mía" (Attias 33.25). The description seems inspired in certain verses of *Conde Claros y el Emperador* (*Yoná 4B*.16−17; Larrea 30.48−51). The great following of maids-in-waiting or knights who accompany a female protagonist is a frequent topic: *Robo de Elena* (Bénichou 91, v. 12); *Expulsión de los judíos de Portugal* (TCR C5.11); *Preferida del rey* (TCR A11.8). The Eastern forms of *Melisenda insomne* tell the following story: The emperor's daughter, Meliselda (Melisselda; Merizelda; Ruzelda; three sisters) cannot sleep (for love of Count Arjelo; Arğile). She tosses about in her bed like a fish in the sea. She leaps out of bed and goes to ask her handmaidens' advice. An ancient crone (one of the sisters) advises her (the others) to enjoy life while she is young. She dresses in finery and goes out into the street. She meets her father's constable or servant boy (Dalmedico, etc.), who reproaches her for being abroad at such an hour. She claims she is going to help a neighbor woman who is in childbirth. She asks to borrow his knife, allegedly to kill the street dogs which are bothering her, and stabs him to death.

Bibliography: Adatto Recordings 11; Algazi 52−53; idem, *Quatre mélodies*, no. 2 (= Algazi); ASK 28(11); Attias 33; Benardete, *JS*, 26(1963), p. 1109, no. 11; idem, *Sheaf*, p. 20; Benmayor 24*a*−24*f*; *Bosnia* C1; CMP B17.1−21; Crews MS IX(vv. 1−6*a*); Danon 7; FRS 9*A*; Gil 18 (= Danon); Hollander 2*A*−2*C*; Lazar 38 (= Levy, I); Levy I, 12.1−6; III, 2; Milner− Storm 6−7 (= Levy, I; Algazi 53); MPelayo 20 (= Danon); PTJ 28, 163 (= Danon; Levy, I); Romey 11; SBS 64−65, 68; SRC PB3, BR22 (BR22 = Danon); UYA 175; Wiener 26.

/Alvar, *Romancero: Tradicionalidad*, p. 404 (= PTJ 28*a*); ASK 28(8); Bénichou 69; Bennaim MS 26; Castro MS 17; CMP B17.22−35; Fereres MS 20; FRS 9*B*; Gil 35 (2d text = MP); Larrea 39−41; Lazar, p. 72 (= PTJ 28*a*); Librowicz (II) B17; MP 28 (= CMP 17.22); MRuiz 39*A*−*B*; Pinto, II.7; PTJ 28*a*−28*b* (28*b* = MRuiz); Thomas, p. 283 (= Bénichou).

///*Primav.* 198; ASW 126 (Todas las gentes dormían/en las que Dios tiene parte). The Eastern *incipit*, "Noche buena, noche buena," can be dated 1684 and 1753 (Avenary, "Cantos," no. 132).

4. *Gaiferos jugador* (*á-e*) (*Gaiferos the Gambler*) (B15) (**Salonika**): Gaifero and Carlo spend their time gambling for silver, gold, and cities. Carlo reproaches his nephew: He has given him Blancaniña (Juliana; Lindaibeya) as his wife and Gaifero, out of cowardice, has allowed her to be carried off. If he does not rescue her, Carlo will put a curse on him: He will suffer hunger, poverty, and other privations wherever he goes in search of her. Gaifero rides off in search of Claraniña.

Benardete's version is essentially identical to Yacob Abraham Yoná's GSA 2, but he alludes to the relationship of his text to a certain *Güerta de historia* also published by Yoná.

Bibliography: ASK 27*a*(1); Attias 26; CMP B15.1−3; Crews MS 12; Díaz-Plaja 11; Mano, p. 52 (= GRI = *Yoná*); Milwitzky, "Viajero," p. 325 (= GSA = *Yoná*); PTJ 27−27*a* (= Attias, Díaz-Plaja); *Yoná* 5.
// AFC 3249; Braga, I, 211−220; Milá 247; VRP 45−49.
///*Primav*. 173; ASW 134−135 (Asentado está Gaiferos/en el palacio real).
See the study by Menéndez Pidal, RoH, I, 286−300, and, for further details, *Yoná* 5.

5. *Rosaflorida y Montesinos* (*í-a*) (*Rosaflorida and Montesinos*) (MP 26/B20) (**Tangier**): Rosaflorida (Rosablanca) lives in a marvelous golden castle, on whose battlements a sapphire shines at night as brilliantly as the sun at midday. She rejects all suitors, but falls in love with Montesinos without ever having seen him. At midnight, the cries of Rosaflorida are heard. A watchman (page) asks her what is wrong. She wishes to send a letter to France to her beloved Montesinos, begging him to come to see her and offering him jewels, a hundred gold *marcos*, a hundred cows, a hundred black slaves, a hundred maids to serve him, a hundred mills, and cloves and cinnamon to flavor his food. If, however, he does not want her, she will offer him her sister, who is more "elegant" (beautiful) than she is. At that moment, Montesinos arrives. Rosaflorida asks him who his father is. He answers that he is the son of a charcoal maker. Rosaflorida faints, but Montesinos reveals that he is really the son of the king of France (of Paris) and grandson (nephew) of the king of Seville (or Castile, Almería, Turkey). They are married.

Bibliography:
/Alvar, *Romancero: Tradicionalidad*, p. 406; ASK 26(6); Bénichou 348; Castro MS 42; CMP B20.1−13; Gallent 4; Larrea 36−38; MP 26 (= CMP B20.1); MRuiz 38; Nahón 6; PTJ 25 (= MRuiz).

//AFC 2236; Milá 257. *A lo divino* versions: FM 68; RPM 371–374.
///*Primav*. 179; ASW 124, 454 (En Castilla está un castillo,/que se llama Rocafrida; En Castilla está un castillo,/al cual dicen Rocha frida; Allá en aquella ribera/que se llama de Ungría).

6. *Juan Lorenzo* (*á*) (*Juan Lorenzo*) (MP 12/C2) (**Salonika**): Juan Lorenzo (Jan Lorencio, Nolencio, etc.) complains that the king wishes to kill him because he has a beautiful wife. Seated at the door of his house, with his wife and children, playing a *vihuela* (*clarineta*), Juan Lorenzo sees the King of Portugal and all his followers approaching over the fields of Arzuma (Ancolores). They greet each other. Juan Lorenzo has a banquet prepared for them. The king strolls in the garden. He plucks a rose and gives it to Juan Lorenzo's wife, saying that in fifteen days she will be queen of Portugal. Juan Lorenzo weeps. The wife urges the king not to kill Juan Lorenzo, but only to have him exiled; she devises a plan so that Juan Lorenzo can visit her, disguised as a charcoal maker; she promises she will kill the king and put Juan Lorenzo in his place. The king appears. The wife seizes his sword and decapitates him. Juan Lorenzo obtains all the king's wealth and reigns in his stead.

Bibliography: ASK 12(2); Attias 3; Besso, "Los sefardíes y el idioma," p. 189; Coello 2; CMP C2.1–11; Crews MS 32; Díaz, *Palabras ocultas*, p. 87; Galante 8; Gil 8 (= Galante; Coello); Luria MS 2.9–18; Mano 40 (= Coello); Manrique de Lara, "Leonor Téllez," p. 299 (= MP); MP 12 (= Coello); Onís 18; PTJ 13 (= Coello).
/ASK 12(18); CMP C2.12–21; Fernández, p. 315 (vv. 6–17); FRS 12; Larrea 11–14; Levy, I, 16; MRuiz 32; Nahón 30.
///The Eastern *incipits*, "Yo estando en la mi puerta" and "Yo me estando en la mi puerta," date from before 1641 and from 1702 respectively. See Avenary, "Cantos," no. 213; Attias, *Cancionero*, p. 361, no. 61. The identification with *Juan Lorenzo* is not certain. On the historical origins of the ballad, see MP 12. Galante's text reflects a radical, probably individual re-elaboration and is not included in our summary. Benardete's version is fragmentary and covers only the initial stages of the narrative. For an abstract of the Moroccan form of *Juan Lorenzo*, see no. 29 *infra*.

7. *La muerte del duque de Gandía* (*í-a*) (*The Death of the Duke of Gandía*) (MP 13/C12) (*7A*. **Gelibolu**; *7B*. **Çanakkale**; *7C*. **Izmir**): In the city of Mesina

(Misía, Marsilia, Veziroglu, Rumeríe), the king circulates a proclamation: Whoever finds the king's son will be given a great sum of money; if he finds him dead, he will be given a reward (or he will be put in his place), and, if he finds him alive, he will be given half the kingdom and the king's daughter as his wife. A poor fisherman appears: He has seen (three) knights throw a mysterious bundle into the river (or the sea). The fisherman drags the river with grappling hooks and cables and pulls out a nobleman, luxuriously dressed and covered with precious stones. The fisherman goes to the king's palace and tells him what he has seen. The king accuses the fisherman of having committed the crime and orders him killed (or sent to the galleys).

Bibliography: Adatto 12; ASK 14(25); Attias 35; Benmayor 2*a*−2*d*, 36*d*; Benmayor, "Oral Narrative," p. 517, n. 29 (= Benmayor 2*a*); CMP C12.1−11; Danon 6; FRS 17*A* (= HBS); Galante 4; Gil 4 (= Galante, Sánchez Moguel); HBS 2 (= TCR); Hollander 3*A*−3*C*; Levy, III, 6; Luria MS 3.5−16; Milwitzky MS 50; MPelayo 18−19 (= Danon; Sánchez Moguel); Onís 27; PTJ 15*a*−15*b* (= Galante; HBS); Romey 21; Sánchez Moguel, *BRAE*, pp. 499−501; SBS 1, 42; TCR C4 (= HBS).
/ASK 14(4); CMP C12.12−22; FRS 17*B*; Gil 4 (= MP); Larrea 15−16; MP 14 (= CMP C12.12); PTJ 15.
///Durán 1251−1252; ASW 36−38 (A veinte y siete de julio,/un lunes, en fuerte día). Benmayor provides a detailed study of the ballad in relation to its historical context.

8. *La expulsión de los judíos de Portugal (í-o)* (*The Exile of the Jews from Portugal*) (MP 13/C13) (**Salonika**): Of the three daughters of King Dolorido (Dolonginos), two are already married; the other one is impatient to find a husband. Messengers arrive with the news that one of her sisters has died and that she is to marry the widower. She is dressed in finery. One hundred maidens and two thousand horsemen accompany her. Moslems, Christians, and Jews go out to meet her. The new queen swears to kill the Jews as soon as she comes to power. Her mother-in-law warns her that, if she involves her son, the king, in her sanguinary plans, she will not be allowed to enter the palace. The queen dies.

Bibliography: ASK 13(2); Attias 57; CMP C13.1−5; FRS 16*A* (= TCR); TCR C5.
/ASK 13(3); Armistead−Silverman, "Aspecto," no. 4 (= Castro); Castro

MS 49; CMP C13.6−13; FRS 16*B* (= Castro); MP 13 (= CMP C13.6);
MRuiz 102; PTJ 14 (= MRuiz).
//Compare ART 257−258; RPC 93; RTCN 115. For a study of the Judeo-
Spanish ballad and its possible relationship to the Castilian texts, see TCR C5.

9. *La muerte del príncipe don Juan (á-a) (The Death of Prince John)* (MP
15/C14) (9*A*. **Salonika**; 9*B*. **Izmir**): The king's son (the king) is ill. The seven
best doctors of Granada look after him. They can do nothing for him. The
"most famous doctor" (or "the one with the woolly beard") has not yet come;
he arrives, riding a black mule and wearing a golden chain (scarf) at his throat;
he has left seven mules and horses dead along the way; he has made a journey of
fifteen days in seven (or seven in four); as he arrives at the door, the mule drops
dead; he goes in to see the sick man. When the latter sees the doctor, he turns
pale. The doctor examines him and states that he has but three hours to live and
an hour and a half has already gone by. Father and mother come in and mourn
for their son. The king's wife enters. Death (el Huerco) appears to claim his
soul. Bells are heard tolling. The king's unborn child will be queen (or king) of
Granada. The king dies at daybreak; the doctor, at dawn.

Bibliography: ASK 15(3); Attias 82; Bassan 16; Cantera Ortiz, p. 22
(= Molho, *Usos*); CMP C14.1−11; ETA 1; FRS 17*A*; Galante 13; Gil 13
(= Galante); Levy, IV, 1−2 (2 = Molho, *Usos*); Lida 2; LSO 178 (= Molho,
Usos); Molho, "Cinq élégies," no. 4; Molho, *Usos*, pp. 269, 330; PTJ 16*a*,
241 (= Galante; Molho, *Usos*); Rodrigo, p. 355; Sojo 6 (= Molho, *Usos*);
SRC ET1 (= ETA).
/Alvar, *Textos*, II, 762; ASK 15(3); Bendayán MS 14; Bénichou 47; Bennaim
MS 108v; CMP C14.12−22; FRS 17*B*; Larrea 17−19; Librowicz (II) C14;
MP 15 (= CMP C14.13); PTJ 16 (= Alvar, *Textos*).
//Braga, I, 627−629; FM 13; RPM 18−25; VRP 6−16.
///Luis Vélez de Guevara's *comedia, La Serrana de la Vera*, dating from 1613,
includes a series of verses from this *romance*. See the ed. by Ramón Menéndez
Pidal and María Goyri de Menéndez Pidal (Madrid: Centro de Estudios Históri-
cos, 1916), pp. 61−62. Bénichou's comparative study of the *romance* in the
various branches of the Hispanic tradition is fundamental (*Creación*, pp.
95−124; on the Jewish versions: pp. 113−117). See also María Goyri de
Menéndez Pidal, "Romance de la muerte del príncipe D. Juan (1497)," *BHi*, 6
(1904), 29−37; Ramón Menéndez Pidal, *El Romancero español* (New York:

Hispanic Society of America, 1910), pp. 100–102 (reproduced in *Estudios sobre el Romancero* [Madrid: Espasa-Calpe, 1973], pp. 66–68); Catalán, "Memoria," pp. 441–443; RoH, II, 291–292.

10. *El nacimiento y vocación de Abraham* (strophic) (*The Birth and Vocation of Abraham*) (MP 30/E3) (**Salonika**): King Nimrod goes out into the fields and sees omens foreshadowing the birth of Abraham. He orders the midwives to kill all newborn male children. Terah's wife flees through the fields and takes refuge in a cave, where Abraham is born. The child speaks at birth. He urges his mother to leave him alone in the cave; angels from heaven will care for him. His mother visits him after eight days and finds him bathing himself. She visits him again in two weeks; he is absorbed in pious studies. After twenty days, she finds a grown young man, looking at the heavens, anxious to know the "God of truth." She asks for Abraham. The young man tells her some wild beast must have devoured Abraham. The mother faints (or weeps). The young man identifies himself as Abraham. He charges his mother to inform Nimrod. The king sends for him. Abraham reproaches him for his lack of faith. Nimrod has a furnace lit and Abraham is thrown in. Angels protect him, fruits grow from the firewood, and Abraham emerges unharmed. Verses in praise of Abraham conclude the poem.

   Bibliography: Algazi 45; ASK 30(4); Attias 127; Bassan 50; *Bosnia*, p. 27; BR 8; CBU, p. 340 (= UR); CMP E3.1–7; Danon 41; Lazar 71 (= UR); Levy, *Antología*, IV, 384–386 (no. 245); LSO 106–111 (nos. 41–43); Mézan, "'Agādôt," p. 205; Milner–Storm 35 (= Algazi + Attias); Molho, "Tres romances," p. 66 (= LSO); MP 30 (= Danon); MPelayo 52 (= Danon); PTJ 32 (= CBU); SBS 125; Simoni 4; SR3; SRC SR3, BR 8; UR, p. 377; Wiener 4, 19.
   /ASK 30(1); CMP E3.8; Librowicz (II) E3; MRuiz 41; PTJ 31 (= MRuiz).

11. *El sacrificio de Isaac (á-o)* (*The Sacrifice of Isaac*) (MP 31/E5) (**Tetuán**): God has tested Abraham nine times. As the tenth test, He asks for his son Isaac as a sacrifice. Abraham takes leave of Sarah and asks for her blessing. She blesses them and tells Abraham to take special care of Isaac, who is still a child. Isaac carries firewood for the sacrifice. He asks Abraham about the ram. He answers: It is God's will that you be the ram. Isaac agrees to be sacrificed, begging his father to bind his hands and feet and cover his eyes. Abraham lifts his knife, but a voice from heaven stays his hand: God has tested his faith. An

informer (or an angel) tells Sarah that Abraham has killed their son. She falls dead. The same informer (or angel) tells Abraham of Sarah's death. Father and son mourn for her, buy a shroud and a grave for Sarah, and bury her in the fields of Hebron (or on Mount Horeb).

Bibliography:

/ASK 31(8); Benoliel, "Ḥakitía," p. 365 (no. 6); Castro MS 38; CMP E5.1−3; García Figueras, p. 697; Larrea 42; Librowicz (II) E5; Milner− Storm 23 (= Larrea); MP 31; MRuiz 42*A*−42*B*; Pinto II.19; PTJ 34−34*a* (34 = MRuiz).

//RPM 1−3; *Por campos*, pp. 56−64.

///*Por campos*, pp. 64−65, 68 (Si se partiera Abraam,/patriarca muy honrado; Ya se parte Abraham). Catalán's study (*Por campos*, pp. 56−75), where he also publishes Moroccan texts from the Archivo Menéndez Pidal (pp. 69−71), is fundamentally important. Note also the Eastern *incipit* dating from 1684 and 1753, "Ya se partea Abraham" (Avenary, "Cantos," no. 206). On the late seventeenth-century Dutch Sephardic version, see also J. Leite de Vasconcellos, "Dois romances peninsulares," *RFE*, 9 (1922), 395−398, and our article, "Three Hispano-Jewish *romances* from Amsterdam," *Medieval and Renaissance Hispanic Studies in Honor of John Esten Keller* (Newark, Delaware, 1981), pp. 243−254.

12. *El robo de Dina* (*ó*) (*The Rape of Dinah*) (MP 32/E7) (**Salonika**): The beautiful Dinah goes walking in the fields of King Hamor (or King Hebron). Because of her twelve brothers, she fears nothing. She approaches a tent, thinking there is no one there. Shechem, the king's son, sees her and speaks to her, praising her beauty. Dinah, indifferent to his advances, answers him by invoking God's protection for her brothers. Shechem approaches her and does "what is not right." Dinah returns home. Jacob (or her twelve brothers) ask(s) her why she is pale. She tells him (them) what has happened. The twelve brothers go off to destroy Shechem's city. Judah demolishes the walls with a stentorian shout. The king delivers his son to them so they can take vengeance upon him.

Except for a minor variation in v. 12, Benardete's text agrees essentially with that of Yacob Abraham Yoná's booklet, *Gu'erta de romansos 'importantes* (GSA, no. 5). See *Yoná* 8.

Bibliography: Amiras MS 27; ASK 32(12); Attias 71; Bassan 18; Besso, "Los sefardíes y el idioma," p. 189; CBU 332 (= UR); CMP E7.1−3; Crews

MS 9; FRS 20; Gil 55 (= MP); Lazar 70 (= UR); LSO 113 (= *Yoná*; except for last verse); Mano 72 (= GRI = *Yoná*); Milner–Storm 29 (= Attias); MP 32 (= GSA = *Yoná*); Onís 30; PTJ 35 (= CBU); SBS 129; UR, p. 367 (= BRI [with minor differences] = *Yoná*); *Yoná* 8.
///Ontañón de Lope, no. 15 (A caça salía Dina,/la hija de[1] gran Jacob); also Frenk Alatorre, "El Cancionero sevillano," p. 359 (no. 1). See our detailed study of the ballad in *Yoná* 8.

13. *Tamar y Amnón (á-a) (Thamar and Amnon)* (MP 37/E17) (**Tangier**): Amnon (Ablón, Ablor, Abnón, etc.), son of King David, falls in love with his own sister, Thamar. He becomes ill and stays in bed. His father goes to see him, asks about his health, and suggests he eat a turkey breast. Amnon answers that he will only eat it if Thamar cooks and serves it to him. Thamar appears and Amnon confesses his love for her. She rejects his advances. He rapes her. She leaves, sad and furious, and meets Absalom. He asks her what has happened and promises to avenge her by shedding Amnon's blood. Amnon is killed. (She marries Amnon.)

Bibliography:
/Alvar, "Amnón y Tamar," nos. 1–4 and pp. 250–251; Armistead–Silverman, "Romancero antiguo," p. 246; ASK 37(27); Attias 74 (= Ortega); Bénichou 113; Castro MS 26; CMP E17.1–11; Essayag MS 17; FRS 22 (= "Romancero antiguo"); Gerson-Kiwi, *Bitfutzot Hagola*, no. 12 (= Ortega); Larrea 45; Lazar 61 (= Alvar, "Amnón y Tamar," no. 1 + no. 3); Librowicz 6; Librowicz (II) E18; Milner–Storm 32 (= Attias + Larrea + Ortega); MP 37 (= CMP E17.1); MRuiz 46 (= Alvar, no. 4); Nahón 11*A*–11*B*; Ortega, p. 218; PTJ 41 (= Alvar, pp. 250–251); Rechnitz 1.
// AFC 3264; FM 23; RPM 4–7; VRP 515–516, 1014. See Alvar's study in *El Romancero: Tradicionalidad*, pp. 165–249.
///Cf. Samuel G. Armistead and Joseph H. Silverman, "Romancero antiguo y moderno (Dos notas documentales)," *AION*, 16 (1974), 245–259: pp. 245–252 (Vn hijo del rey David/namoró se de su hermana).

14. *Blancaflor y Filomena (é-a) (Blancaflor and Filomena)* (MP 100/F1) (14*A*. **Salonika**; 14*B*. **Izmir**): The king's son has served the king for seven years in order to win Felismena (Ferijmena, Felismení, Ferismena) and is dying of love for her, but they marry him to Miraibella (Sanjiguela) instead. He leaves

to go to war. On returning, he stops at his mother-in-law's house and tells her that her daughter is to have a child. He begs her to accompany him, so that she can be with her daughter; but if the mother-in-law herself cannot go, he asks that Felismena go in her stead, promising (swearing on his sword) to care for her and treat her with courtesy. He puts her on his horse and, along the way, attempts to make love to her. Felismena rejects him. He throws her off the horse, rapes her, and cuts out her tongue. With her own blood, Felismena writes a letter to her father (and mother) and gives it to a page (a young man; an old man; a count), who happens to be passing by. The old man takes her to her parents. As soon as she arrives at home, she [*read* Miraibella] gives birth to a child. She makes a stew of the child's body and serves it to "the father"[i.e., the king's son, her husband]. He exclaims that the meal is delicious. [The mother-in-law answers:] "Eat, son-in-law, for you are eating your own flesh."

Bibliography: Adatto 4; Adatto Recordings 29; ASK 100(1); Attias 37; Coello 3; CMP F1.1−7; Crews MS 18; Díaz-Plaja 10; Galante 9; Gil 9 (= Galante, Coello); Milwitzky MS 5, 40, 52; SBS 24−25.
/ASK 100(7); Bénichou 247, CMP F1.8−15; Gil 9 (= MP); Larrea 150; Librowicz (II) F1; MP 100 (= CMP F1.8); MRuiz 81.
//AFC 3161; Beutler 16; Braga, I, 598−606; FM 24; Milá 270; RPM 177−178.

15. *Hero y Leandro* (ó) + *La malcasada del pastor* (ó) (*Hero and Leander* + *The Shepherd's Mismated Wife*) (MP 41/F2 + MP 72/L8) (**Izmir**): Vv. 1−14 represent *Hero y Leandro*: Of three sisters, two are married and the youngest is "in perdition." Her father, out of shame, sends her to France (Rhodes, Rogos, Rogas, Aragón, Romi, etc.) and builds her a castle of fine stones, pearls, coral, and plaster in the middle of the sea and without doors, balconies, or windows, so no man can come in. Her lover finds out and throws himself into the sea, swimming (he made oars of his arms and of his body a ship) and calling to her by name (Cara-de-flor; Blancaflor). She is asleep, but recognizes his voice and throws down her tresses so he can climb up into the castle. She washes his hands and feet, seats him in a golden chair, gives him a change of clothes and a dinner, including fish, with lemon, meat, and prunes with rice, almonds, love apples, and wine. She makes up a fine bed for him and they go to bed together.

Bibliography: Adatto MS 3; Adatto Recordings 6; ASK 41(25); Attias 61; Attias, "Çĕrôr," no. 18; Baruch, p. 279; Benmayor 4a−4d; *Bosnia* B3, C2 (B3 = Baruch); CMP F2.1−18; Crews MS 23, IV; Estrugo, *Los sefardíes*,

p. 137; Estrugo, "Reminiscencias," pp. 74–75; Estrugo, "Tradiciones," p. 145; FRS 24; Galante 3; Gil 3 (= Galante); Giménez Caballero D; Hemsi 33; Hollander 5A–5B; Lazar 62 (= Baruch); Levy, I, 4–5; II, 8–9; IV, 4–5; LSO, p. 84; Milner–Storm 13 (= Levy, II, 8); Milwitzky MS 25, 49, 53, 58; Moya, II, 258; MP 41 (= Galante); PTJ 45, 45a–45b (= Galante; *Bosnia* B3; Levy, I, 4); Romey 10; Simoni 2; Torner, *Temas folklóricos*, pp. 57–58. All Sephardic versions contaminated by *La malcasada del pastor* are brought together in RLH, IX, 325–346; see also pp. 279–280.

////Other European traditions include ballads that seem to be distantly related to *Hero y Leandro*: Child 216 (*The Mother's Malison* or *Clyde's Water*); Doncieux, pp. 280–294 (*Le flambeaux d'amour*); DVM, I, 20 (*Die Königskinder*); Nigra 7 (*Ero e Leandro*).

Vv. 15–24 pertain to *La malcasada del pastor*: A young girl, the only (or spoiled) daughter of parents from France (Brusa) and Aragon (Istanbul, Anatolia), is married to the best among all the shepherds (or a rich lord; a young man; a European; a count). He eats meat, fish, hazel nuts, and fine (fresh) bread, drinks wine, and sleeps on a (high) bed; she is given bones, nut shells, black bread (crusts or crumbs), water, and a mat (boards, the floor, a low bed) to sleep on. He beats her. To test her fidelity, he sends her at midnight (at dawn) on a tiring walk to a distant fountain (to the river) to fetch water. Her jug breaks along the way. The running water lulls her to sleep beside the fountain. A knight (young man; traveler; three young men; three knights) pass(es) by, praise(s) her beauty, touch(es) her face, and give(s) her three (seven) kisses (pinch(es) her three times). She wakes up and exclaims: "If my husband finds out, I'll be killed." She threatens to kill herself. The knight identifies himself as her husband (or her "beloved"), tells her not to be frightened, and says that he wanted to test her. They return home. (Below we list only "autonomous" versions, uncontaminated with *Hero y Leandro*.)

Bibliography: Adatto MS 12; ASK 72(11); Attias, "Çĕrôr," no. 9; Benmayor 16a-16b; *Bosnia* C10; CMP L8.1–12; Crews MS V; Danon 33; FRS 46; Galante 3 (=Danon); Gil 3 (= Danon); Hemsi 50; Hollander 5A–5B; Levy, I, 1; II, 18–20; Luria MS 8; MacCurdy, p. 232; Milner–Storm 88 (=Levy, II, 19); Milwitzky MS 12, 48, 74; MP 72; MPelayo 44 (= Danon); PTJ 71 (= Danon); Romey 9; SBS 98; SRC BR25 (= Danon); Wiener 9.

/Bénichou 134; Castro MS 41 (= RLH, IX, no. IV.75); CMP L8.13–19; Gil 3, 3rd text (= MP); Larrea 100; MP 72 (= CMP L8.13); PTJ 71a (= Bénichou). Sephardic versions from both traditions, including the extensive contaminations present in *Hero y Leandro* and various other *romances*, are brought together in RLH, IX, 293–353; see also pp. 275–284.

//For Catalan versions, in which the shepherd undergoes privations while the wife lives well, see RLH, IX, 281–283.

See no. 29 *infra* for an abstract of the Moroccan form of *La malcasada del pastor*.

16. *El robo de Elena (á-o)* (*The Abduction of Helen of Troy*) (MP 43/F5) (**Salonika**): Queen Izelda (Izela) is embroidering a love banner; her scissors, thread, thimble, and needle fall to the ground and she goes down to retrieve them. Parizi (Parizis, Paricia, Pariste), her lover, passes by. He greets her and she asks him who he is and what his trade is. He answers that he is a merchant and notary (or corsair). He has three (one, two, six, seven) ship(s) in port (in the gulf), with golden (crystal) rudders, silk rigging, and silver (silken, golden) sails; they are loaded with precious materials. In one of them there is an apple tree (lemon tree) which yields apples of love (golden apples) in winter and summer. Izelda is anxious to see the tree. Parizi invites her to his ship. She dresses in finery and arrives at the boat. As soon as she steps on board, Parizi hoists the sails, raises the anchor, and sails away with her (to France). Izelda wonders why the boat is moving; she evokes the husband and child she has left behind; she asks about the apple tree. Parizi consoles her: the wind is moving the boat; he is (or she is) the apple tree; the apples are the children she will bear him.

V. 17 of Benardete's version is a contamination from *El falso hortelano*. See *Yoná* 21A.11.

Bibliography: Adatto 2; Adatto Recordings 16; ASK 43(14); Attias 6; Catalán, *Por campos*, pp. 107–109; Benmayor 25a-25b; CBU, pp. 330–331 (= UR); CMP F5.1–17; Crews MS 34; Danon 2; Díaz-Plaja 14; FRS 26A; Gil 29 (= Danon); Hemsi, "Evocation," pp. 1092–1093 (= *Yoná* 11B); Mano, p. 58 (= GRI + Danon); Milwitzky MS 7, 22, 33; Milwitzky, "Viajero," p. 326 (= GSA); MPelayo 14 (= Danon); Onís 37; PTJ 46 (= Danon); Romey 16; Sciaky, p. 37; UR, p. 1 (= GRI); *Yoná* 11A-11B. /ASK 43(9); Bénichou 91; Bennaim MS 72; Castro MS 52; Catalán, *Por campos*, pp. 110–111; CMP F5.18–26; FRS 26B; Gil, p. lxxiii (= MP); Larrea 47–49; Librowicz (II) F5; MP 43 (= CMP F5.18); MRuiz 48; Nahón 12; PTJ 46a (= Bénichou); Thomas, p. 284 (= Bénichou). //FM 1. ///*Primav.* 109 (Reina Elena, Reina Elena,/¡Dios prospere tu estado!). Note

the Eastern incipits, "Estábase reina Elena" (1594) and "Estaba la reina
Elena" (1704) (Avenary, "Cantos," no. 81; Attias, *Cancionero*, p. 362,
no. 25). Catalán's study (*Por campos*, pp. 101−117) is of fundamental importance; see also Bénichou 91 and Nahón 12.
////Needless to say DgF, VIII, no. 467 (*Paris og Dronning Ellen*) is related
only through its similar dependence on medieval Troy narratives.

17. *Tarquino y Lucrecia (á-a) (Tarquin and Lucrece)* (MP 45/F7) (**Salonika**):
Tarquino(s) (Tarkindo, Katirvo, Ferdino), king of the Romans, falls in love
with Lucrecia (Lucreza, Ducquerencia; the queen). He disguises himself as a
traveler and passes by her door. Lucrecia receives him like a king. She washes
his hands and feet, seats him in a golden chair, serves him dinner, and makes up
a golden bed, with an embroidered blanket, for him to sleep in. Tarquino
awakes at midnight and goes to Lucrecia's bed (or room). He puts a dagger to
her breast. He tells her that, if she grants him her love, she will be queen (of
Granada); if not, he will kill her and will also kill one of her black slaves (an old
man), place the body in her bed, and see to it that the scandal is known
throughout Rome. Lucrecia answers that she would rather die honorably than
live in dishonor. She does not want "her people" to say that she was married to
a Christian. Tarquino kills her with his sword (knife).
    V. 6 is a contamination from *El Forzador* (No. 32 *infra*).
    Bibliography: Adatto 10; Adatto Recordings 2, 17; ASK 45(2); Attias,
"Ha-rômansah *Tarkînôs*," pp. 98−101; Benmayor 5; CBU, p. 334 (= UR);
Coello 1; CMP F7.1−2; FRS 27; Gil 15 (= Coello); Hollander 6*A*−6*B*; PTJ
47−47*a* (= Coello, UR); Romey 20; UR, no. 5, p. 368.
/ASK 45(1); Bénichou 95; CMP F7.3−9; Gil 15 (2d text) (= MP); Larrea 50;
Librowicz (II) F7; MP 45 (= CMP F7.9); Nahón 13.
//Braga, I, 597−598.
///Durán 519 (Aquel rey de los romanos / que Tarquino se llamaba). Note also
the Eastern *incipit*: "Aquel rey de los romancos" dated 1684 (Avenary,
"Cantos", no. 16). See Suzanne Petersen, "Cambios estructurales en el
Romancero tradicional," *El Romancero en la tradición oral moderna*, ed.
Diego Catalán, Samuel G. Armistead, and Antonio Sánchez Romeralo (Ma-
drid: C.S.M.P., 1972), pp. 167−179: 177−178; Nahón 13; and our note,
"Una variación antigua del romance de *Tarquino y Lucrecia*," *BICC*, 33
(1978), 122−126.

18. *Virgilios (é) (Virgil)* (MP 46/F8) (**Salonika**): Virgil (Vergil, Vergiles,
Virgile, Doverdjeli, Argiles, Vergino, Duvergini) is imprisoned for treason

because he made love to a girl (Zadé, Zaïdé, Sadé, Zadem), the king's niece. The king has him put into a deep dungeon, to which the king himself carries the keys. Time passes and no one remembers Virgil, except his mother, who visits him every day (and brings him food). One day, on his way to mass (or at mass; at the window), the king sees a woman pass by dressed in mourning. He is informed that it is Virgil's mother (or wife [!]; the king's niece), dressed in mourning for Virgil, who is chained in prison. He orders all of his knights (his slaves) to finish saying mass quickly, to prepare tables (dinner), and to sit down to dinner, after which (or in the meantime), they will go to see Virgil. The queen refuses to eat (or to say mass) without him. They all go to visit Virgil in prison. The king inquires as to his condition and is told that he is combing his hair and his beard, which had just begun to grow when he entered prison and are now turning grey (or his beard has reached his feet); his fingernails have grown to three palms' lengths; his eyelashes are so long that he cannot see; Virgil has been in prison seven (fifteen) years, yet he patiently offers to stay for ten (or sixteen) years more. The king summons his knights and they take Virgil off to the baths (or to dinner) and shave him, after which he is given the royal crown, the king's clothes, and the king's horses. He is married to the king's niece.

Bibliography: Adatto Recordings 26; ASK 46(6); Attias 7; Attias, "Çĕrôr," no. 19; Baruch, p. 277; Bidjarano, p. 24*a*; *Bosnia* A1, B1, C3 (B1 = Baruch); CMP 58.1–27; Danon 15; Gil 50 (= Danon); González-Llubera 1; LSO, p. 73; Milwitzky MS 36; MPelayo 27 (= Danon); Onís 43; PTJ 48*a* (= Baruch); Pulido, p. 296.

/Alvar, "Romances de *La bella*," pp. 266–270; ASK 46(15); Bénichou 99; Castro MS 16; CMP F8.28–36; Fereres MS 10; FRS 28; Gil 53 (= MP); Larrea 51–53; Librowicz (II) F8; Librowicz, "Gibraltar," no. 2; MP 46 (= CMP F8.28); MRuiz 49; Nahón 14*A*–14*C*; PTJ 48 (= Alvar, "Romances de *La bella*").

//RPC 125; RTCN 114; VRP 293.

///*Primav.* 111; Nahón 14, n. 1; RoH, I, 347 (Mandó el rey prender a Virgilios / y a buen recaudo poner; Mandā tomar a Uirgilius / a buē recaudo poner). See R. Menéndez Pidal, "Un episodio de la fama de Virgilio en España," *SMe*, 5 (1932), 332–341: pp. 332–333. Note also a sixteenth-century *a lo divino* version, "Preso estaua el primer honbre, / que Dios le mandó prender." See Harold G. Jones, "El cancionero español (*Cod. Reg. Lat.* 1635) de la *Biblioteca Vaticana*," *NRFH*, 21 (1972), 370–392: no. 155.

19. *Las hermanas reina y cautiva (í-a)* (*The Two Sisters: Queen and Captive*) (MP 48/H1) (**Tetuán**): The Moslem queen, Xerifa (Sefira, Jalifiana), who lives

in Almería (Almedina), sends her Moorish raiders to France and England to capture a Christian slave girl. They find Count Flores (Flor, Claros, Niño) praying for an heir to inherit his estate; they kill him and capture his wife. They present her to the queen. The countess is sent to work in the pantry and the kitchen. The queen and the captive are both with child and give birth on the same day. The queen bears a daughter; the captive, a son. The midwives, to earn money, switch the children. One day the queen overhears the captive singing to the infant girl: "If you were my daughter and were in my own country, I would call you Blancaflor, which was my sister's name. She was carried off by the Moors on Easter Day while gathering flowers in the gardens (fields) of Almería." The queen asks her to repeat the song and to describe her sister. She answers that she had a mole below her breast (on her left shoulder; on her side). The sisters recognize each other, embrace, exchange children, and return by boat to their homeland. (The queen sends her sister home; marries her sister to the greatest noble of Seville; both sisters die of emotion.)

V. 27 of Benardete's version represents a contamination from *Diego León*. (See Nahón 26*A*.33.) The reading "por la gran desdicha suya" ('. . . mía'), in v. 13*b*, offers an interesting Moroccan example of a phenomenon more frequently encountered in the Eastern tradition. This might be termed the "euphemistic third person" used instead of the first person to avoid connecting the speaker with some unpleasant or unfortunate feature of the narrative. This may also be the case in 22.3*a*: "¿Si has visto a su marido . . . ?" ('. . . mi marido'), which is also from Tetuán. For various Eastern examples, see TCR, no. C3, n. 15; CMP, III, 340, s.v. *allá*.

Bibliography: Adatto 3; Adatto Recordings 20; Algazi 47; ASK 48(4); Attias 11; Attias, "Çĕrôr," no. 1 (= González-Llubera); Baruch, p. 283; Benmayor 11*a*−11*d*; *Bosnia* B11, C4 (B11 = Baruch); CMP H1.1−9; Crews MS 14, XI; Danon 21; FRS 30*A*; Galante 7; Gil 7 (= Galante; Danon); González-Llubera 2; Hollander 8; Katz, "Ladino Literature"; Levy, II, 4; III, 44; MPelayo 32 (= Danon); Romey 17−17*A*.

/Alvar, "Cinco romances," no. 1; idem, *Romancero: Tradicionalidad*, p. 405 (= PTJ 50*b*); ASK 48(19); Bénichou 219; Castro MS 46; CMP H1.10−20; Fernández, p. 321; FRS 30*B*; Gallent 3; Gil 7, 3rd text (= MP); Larrea 54−57; Larrea, "Romances hispánicos," p. 52 (= Larrea 55); Levy, IV, 3; Librowicz 7; Librowicz (II) H1; MP 48 (= CMP H1.10); MRuiz 50; Ortega 225; Pinto 8; PTJ 50*b* (= Alvar, "Cinco romances"); Pulido, p. 54 (= MP).

//AFC 3028; Braga, II, 128−136, 144−146; FM 29; Milá 242, 242.1; RPM 205−208; VRP 630−639.

///Cf. Child 62 (*Fair Annie*); DgF, no. 258 (*Skjøn Anna*). See *JVF*, 19 (1974), 159 (concerning p. 133); Bénichou, pp. 219–226. The connection with the medieval romance, *Flore et Blanchefleur*, remains to be studied in detail.

20. *Don Bueso y su hermana* (strophic) (*Don Bueso and His Sister*) (MP 49/H2) (20*A*. **Salonika**): A girl (Blancaniña, Blancailinda) is abducted by the Moors. "From the high seas," she is brought in, covered with jewels. She is wearing a sapphire that shines like the sun at midday. The Moor who has carried her off is happy; her mother, the queen, is sad. The girl is taken before the Moorish queen (the King of France; of Alexandra; King Nelmoro), who claims she does not want the captive, fearing the young king will be attracted by her beauty. The girl is deprived of wine and given menial tasks, in the hope that her beauty will fade, but she only becomes more beautiful under harsh treatment. She is sent to the river to wash clothes early in the morning. A knight (young man; count), her brother, Don Buezo (Dombezo; Dumbelo; Alborto; the count) rides by. He is returning from the war and his weapons are stained with blood. He notes the similarity between the girl's white hands and beautiful feet and those of his sister. He asks her to go away with him. She agrees (and says that, if he is her brother, she expects him to take her to Franquía). He asks her if she wishes to ride behind the saddle or on it. She answers that, because of her lineage, she should ride on the saddle. She asks what she should do with the clothes she is washing. He tells her to take along the valuable clothes, but leave those of little value in the river. As they ride along, she recognizes the fields of olive trees (belonging to her father, King Alegsandra), which she knew as a child. The knight realizes she is his sister (Zafira). Their mother joyfully welcomes her long-lost daughter. The mother, or both mother and daughter, die(s) of joy.

(20*B*: **Tetuan**): On Easter Monday, the Moors attack the fields of Oliva (Olivar) and carry off Blancaniña together with other captives. They give her to the Moorish queen, who claims she does not want the captive, fearing the young king will be attracted by her beauty. She is given menial tasks, in the hope that her beauty will fade, but she only becomes more beautiful under harsh treatment. She is sent to the river to wash clothes. A knight, her brother, Don Güezo (Don Flora; the king's son), rides by and notes the similarity between her white hands and beautiful feet and those of his sister. He asks her to go away with him. She asks what she should do with the clothes she is washing. He tells her to take along the valuable clothes, but leave those of little value in the river. As they ride along, she recognizes the fields of olive trees she knew as a child and where she had accompanied her brother and her father the king. The knight realizes she is his sister. Their mother joyfully welcomes her long-lost daughter and offers her son the fields of Oliva and Holanda as a reward for bringing the good news.

The reference to "la reina Izela" (20*A*.6) is a contamination from *El robo de Elena* (see no. 16 *supra*). Compare LSO, p. 69, vv. 5−6.

Bibliography: Adatto 1; Adatto Recordings 22, 26*a*; ASK 49(32); Attias 1; Attias, "Ha-rômansah šel Don Bu'ezo"; Benmayor 27*a*−27*j*; *Bosnia* C5; CMP H2.1−31; Crews MS 11; Danon 18; Díaz-Plaja 2; DRH 8 (= TCR A8); Estrugo, *Los sefardíes*, p. 127; Estrugo, "Reminiscencias," p. 71; Estrugo, "Tradiciones," p. 144; FRS 31*A*; Gil 46 (= Danon); Granell, p. 292; Hemsi 25; Hemsi, "Evocation," p. 1056*b*; Hollander 9*A*−9*D*; Kaludova, p. 106; Katz D; Levy, I, 10; II, 1−3; LSO, p. 69; MacCurdy, text H; Milner−Storm 1−2 (= Attias + Levy, II, 2; Levy, II, 3); Milwitzky MS 2, 44; MPelayo 29 (= Danon); PTJ 51−51*b* (= Danon; Levy, I, 10; Díaz-Plaja); Romey 15; RoH, I, 401; Salavin 1; SBS 20, 23; TCR A8 (= DRH); Valls 8 (= Levy, I, 10).

/Alvar, "Cinco romances," p. 75, n. 60; ASK 49(20); Bénichou 239; Bennaim MS 36; Castro MS 29; CMP H2.32−40; Fereres MS 7−8; Fernández, p. 320; FRS 31*B*; Gil 45 (= MP); Larrea 58−60, 229; Larrea, "Romances hispánicos," p. 52 (= Larrea 58); Librowicz 8 and p. 50; Librowicz (II) H3; MP 49 (= CMP H2.32); MRuiz 51*A*−51*B*; Nahón 16*A*−16*B*; PTJ 51*c*−51*d* (51*c* = Bénichou).

Bénichou, Bennaim, Fereres, Fernández, Larrea 59−60, Librowicz 8, Librowicz (II), MRuiz 51*A*.22ff. and 51*B*, PTJ 51*d*, and a majority of the texts we have collected from Moroccan informants represent the modern octosyllabic Peninsular form of *Don Bueso*. (See CMP H3.1−5.) They have not been taken into account in our summary.

//AFC 2324; Beutler 20; FM 28, 28*bis*; Milá 250; RPM 189−193 and 194−204.

////DgF, VI, nos. 378 and 381 (*Den genfundne Søster; Svend og hans Søster*); DVM, I, no. 4; IV, no. 72 (*Die Meererin; Südeli* or *Die wiedergefundene Schwester*). See the indispensable study by Ramon Menéndez Pidal, "Supervivencia del *Poema de Kudrun* (Orígenes de la balada)," *Los godos y la epopeya española* (Madrid: Austral, 1956), pp. 89−173 (reprinted from *RFE*, XX, 1933), or the German version, "Das Fortleben des Kudrungedichtes (Der Ursprung der Ballade)," *JVF*, 5 (1936), 85−122 (now reprinted in *Probleme der Volksballadenforschung* [Darmstadt: Wissenschaftliche Buchgesellschaft, 1975], pp. 138−193); also DRH 8; TCR A8; Nahón 16.

21. *La vuelta del marido* (í) (*The Husband's Return*) (MP 58/I1) (**Izmir**): Amadí's lady sits combing her hair with an ivory (crystal) comb on the highest branch of a marvelous tree, which has golden roots and an ivory base (branches). A noble knight, who looks like Amadí (Amadín, Amavdín, Amadil) comes riding by and asks the lady what she is looking for. She asks him if he has seen her husband, Amadí, who departed for the war and has not returned. The knight says he knows him well and is bringing a letter from him. He asks what she would give in exchange for being able to see Amadí. The lady makes a series of offers. She will give him her three mills, three fields, three mansions, three palaces, three cities, three brushes, three cows, three tresses, Amadí's sword and lance, two thousand ducats, three doubloons, three young men, and her three daughters, but the knight always asks for more. He will only settle for possessing her. She curses him. He then identifies himself as her husband. She asks for a sign. He (or she) has a mole (three golden hairs) below his (or her) left breast (armpit). (She throws down her tresses for a ladder, so he can climb up to her. They embrace, go home together, and go to bed.)

Bibliography: Adatto 7a-7b; Adatto MS 6; Adatto Recordings 7a; Algazi 65; Id., *Quatre Mélodies* (= Algazi); Armistead–Sala–Silverman, "Un último eco," pp. 235–236; ASK 58(39); Attias 20; Attias, "Çĕrôr," no. 12; Bar-Lewaw, p. 2119 (1st text = Tarica); Baruch, p. 280; Baruch, *Izabrana djela*, p. 275 (= Danon); Behar, p. 29; Benmayor 28a–28i; *Bosnia* B6, C7; CMP I1.1–24; Danon 17; Díaz-Plaja 1; FRS 34; Gerson-Kiwi, *Bitfutzot hagola*, no. 13; Gil 52 (= Danon); Haboucha 1; Hollander 11A–11C; Jungić 1; Katz A; Katz, *WF*, 21, pp. 87–89; Kayserling, p. xi; Lazar, p. 52 (= Díaz-Plaja); Levy, I, 7–8; II, 13; IV, 8; LSO, p. 83; Luria MS 5A–5B; MacCurdy, text A; Mano, p. 32 (= Danon); Milner–Storm 16 (= Levy, II, 13); Milwitzky MS 13, 20, 65; MP 58 (2d text = Wiener); MPelayo 28 (= Danon); Noga Alberti, *Comunidades*, pp. 257–259; Onís 46; PTJ 57–57a (= Baruch, Díaz-Plaja); Romano, p. 601; Romey 19; SBS 76; SICh 6 (= TCR B6); *Spomenica*, p. 321 (= Baruch); Tarica, p. 3; TCR B6 (= SICh); Wiener 8.

/ASK 58 (3); CMP I1.25–28; Essayag MS 1–5; MRuiz 78b.5–7.

//Braga, I, 35–50, 52–69; Carré, nos. 60, 62; RPC 60; VRP 295–344. See also NSR, p. 71, n. 44; TCR B6, nn. 23–24.

///The Eastern *incipits*, "Arbolera tan gentil" and "Arbolera, arbolera, /arbolera tan ğentil," dated from 1555 and 1702 respectively, attest to the ballad's early traditionality. See Avenary, "Cantos," no. 20; Attias, *Cancionero*, p. 363, no. 8. The first extensive Sephardic text dates from 1794 (Attias, "Çĕrôr," no. 12). *La vuelta del marido* (í) probably contaminated the Car-

olingian *romance* of *Almerique de Narbona* (*í*) (Del Soldán de Babilonia / desse os quiero decir [*Primav.* 196; Rodríguez-Moñino, *Cancionero de romances,* 1550, p. 318]). See TCR B6, n. 30.
////Decombe, pp. 214—221; Rolland, I, 220—223 (*Le prisonnier de Hollande*). For more French texts, see "Un último eco," p. 235, n. 7; TCR B6, n. 34.

22. *La vuelta del marido (é) (The Husband's Return)* (MP 59/I2) (**Tetuán**): The wife tells a passing soldier to stop his horse and thrust his lance into the ground. She asks him if he is returning from the wars. He says he is returning from the wars with the English (or: The soldier is leaving for France and offers to do whatever errand the lady may wish). The lady asks him if he has seen her husband. The soldier says he does not know him and asks for a description. The wife says that her husband is blond and tall as a cypress tree, he rides a white horse and bears the king's insignia on his lance (or sword). According to the soldier, the husband died a month before, stating in his will that the soldier should marry his wife. She refuses categorically. She will wait for seven (or fourteen) years and then she and her three (two) daughters will become nuns. The soldier walks three times around the palace without being recognized and then identifies himself as her husband. He throws himself at her feet. Hand in hand they go up into their "arbor."

Vv. 16—18 of Benardete's version are *Wanderstrophen* which occur in other contexts in both the Eastern Sephardic, Spanish, and Hispano-American traditions. See Rechnitz, p. 128, n. 17; Nahón, no. 21, n. 3; also Adolfo Ernst, "Para el cancionero popular venezolano," *Archivos Venezolanos de Folklore* (Caracas), 8 (1967), 75—80: p. 78. Vv. 21—22 are also migratory and serve as the *dénouement* of other Judeo-Spanish ballads: *Vuelta del marido (í)* (CMP I1.27—28); *Conde Niño* (CMP J1.18); *Repulsa y compasión* (Larrea 171.15—18). Compare, in *Conde Claros y la infanta* (Media noche era por filo, / los gallos querían cantar): "Tomárala por la mano, / para un vergel se van; // a la sombra de un aciprés, / debajo de un rosal . . ." (*Primav.* 190.46—47). On the magical circumambulation in v. 19, see our note, "'Siete vueltas dio al castillo . . .'," *RDTP*, 30 (1974), 323—326.

Bibliography: ASK 59(8); Attias 18; FRS 35*A* (= NSR); Hemsi 35; Levy, II, 5—7; NSR, p. 69; PTJ 58 (= Attias); Salavin 5; SBS 96.
/ASK 59(13); Bénichou 227; Castro MS 8; CMP I2.1—9; Fereres MS 11; Fernández, p. 317; FRS 35*B*; Larrea 74—77; Levy, I, 15; Librowicz 10;

Librowicz (II) I2; Librowicz, "Gibraltar," no. 5; MP 59 (= CMP I2.1); MRuiz 68; Nahón 21; Ortega 212; PTJ 58*a* (= MRuiz); Rechnitz 3; Thomas, p. 290 (= Bénichou).
//Beutler 18; FM 47; RPM 114−117.
///*Primav.* 156 (Caballero de lejas tierras, / llegáos acá y paréis).
////Gaston Paris, *Chansons du XVe. siècle* (Paris: Firmin−Didot, 1875), pp. 127−128 (Gentilz gallans de France / qui en la guerre allez). See also Bénichou, p. 229, n. 1.

23. *El conde Niño (á) (The Persecuted Lovers)* (MP 55/J1) (23A. **Salonika**): Count Alimán (Alimar, Alemale, Alimá, Almán, Alemare) walks along the seashore and sings a marvelous song (or: A nightingale sings a glorious song on a rose bush, with golden roots and a crystal base or leaves, growing in the queen's garden). The queen is embroidering and the princess is sleeping. The queen tells her daughter to wake up and come to her chamber at night to hear the beautiful singing of the mermaid of the sea. The daughter answers: "It is not the mermaid, but rather Count Alimar (or a young man), who is courting me. He can court me (or sing) night and day, but he shall not win me." The mother says she will order him killed. The daughter protests that, if he is to be killed, she also wishes to die. The queen orders them both (or only the young man) killed. They are transformed consecutively into plants (carnation and rose bush or carnation plant; citron and citron tree); a dove and a hawk; fishes (perch, flounder, spiny fish, "black fish"; and black carp, grey mullet) in the sea (or pearls and coral). Each time, the wicked queen pulls them up or kills them. They turn into a serpent and a scorpion, which kill the queen (or the fish bones stick in her throat and she chokes; or they become flowers, whose smell kills her).

(23B. **Tangier**): On St. John's morning, Count Niño goes along the seashore to water his horses. He sings a marvelous song, which produces supernatural effects: pregnant women abort, mountains and valleys come together, doors open, travelers return home, birds alight to listen (or fly out of their nests), fretful children go to sleep (or sleeping children wake). The queen tells her daughter, the princess, to wake up and hear the beautiful singing of the mermaid of the sea. The daughter answers: "It is not the mermaid, but rather it is Count Niño who is courting me (dying of love for me)." The mother says she will order him killed. The daughter protests that, if he is to be killed, she wishes to be buried together with him. The queen orders them killed. They are buried together and are transformed into trees (citron and lemon), which grow from their graves. The queen has them cut down. Blood and milk flow from her and royal blood from him. They then become a dove and a hawk, which fly up to heaven. The wicked queen has them killed. But the next day, the queen does not appear in her usual place (or she dies within three days).

V. 9 of Benardete's text 23*A* is taken from *El conde Alemán y la reina*; 12 – 13 are shared by many Salonikan versions of both ballads, but probably belong originally to *El conde Alemán y la reina*, as also does the count's name in the Eastern version of *Niño*. (See *Yoná*, p. 112, n. 5.) *Conde Niño* in the Eastern tradition has diversified into various quite different sub-types, all details of which have not been included in the present abstract. In the Bosnian tradition (*Bosnia*; CMP J1.1 – 4, 6; Crews MS; Levy, III, 48), the *manseviko* alone apparently suffers the first transformation: He is burned to death; the ashes are thrown into the sea and change into pearls and coral; the girl rushes to save him; they turn into a dove and a hawk respectively; they alight on the pasha's palace and the vizier's mansion, where there is a thorn tree, "Que no los dešava gozar (bevir)." Some unedited Rhodian versions are also aberrant: Here three youths undergo consecutive transformations to citrons, apples, flatfish (*chapuras*) or doves, fish, carnations. (Concerning all these transformations, see *Yoná*, pp. 160 – 161, 164.) Such presumably older variations have been largely replaced in most Eastern sub-traditions by a radically abbreviated and contaminated (with *Hero y Leandro*) fragment, diffused, at least in part, by means of popular phonograph recordings. To this sub-type belong Benmayor 22; CBU; CMP J1.5, 7 – 8, 15 – 16, 18, 20; Hemsi, "Sur le folklore," Var. 2; Hollander; Levy, III, 46; Milwitzky; RoH; Romey; San Sebastián; SBS 36. In the Moroccan tradition, the ballad's local Sephardic form is often joined to details taken from Peninsular versions, which are also sung in their entirety in the local tradition, as in the case of Alvar, Larrea 67, and Librowicz. Béni-chou's commentary is fundamental. See also Nahón, p. 97.

Bibliography: Adatto 5 (= GRA, with minor variants); Adatto Recordings 1; ASK 55(19); Attias 16; Baruch, p. 278; Benmayor 22; *Bosnia* B2, C6 (B2 = Baruch); CBU, pp. 339 – 340 (= UR); Coello 6; CMP J1.1 – 20; Crews MS X; Danon 19; Díaz-Plaja 9; FRS 39*A*; Galante 2; Gil 2 (= Galante, Danon, Coello); Hemsi 37; Hemsi, "Sur le folklore," pp. 794 – 795; Hollander 12*A* – 12*C*; Levy, I, 20.1 – 2; III, 46, 48; Lida 1; Mano, p. 22 (= Galante); Milwitzky MS 47; MPelayo 30 (= Danon); PTJ 54 – 54*c* (= Coello, Díaz-Plaja, Danon, Baruch); RoH, I, 401; Romey 3; San Sebastián 1 (III); SBS 35 – 36;

SRC SR6, BR12, BR21 (SR = GRA; BR12 = SR; BR21 = Danon); UR 10;
Yoná 12.
/Alvar, "Cinco romances," no. 2; ASK 55(17); Bénichou 123; Bennaim MS
60, 66; Castro MS 44; CMP J1.21−35; Essayag MS 14−16; FRS 39*B*; Gil, pp.
xx−xxi (= MP); Larrea 67−69; Levy, I, 18; Librowicz 11; Librowicz (II) J1;
Librowicz, "Gibraltar," no. 3; Milner−Storm 8 (= Levy, I, 18 + Larrea
67 + Bénichou); Moya, II, 256; MP 55 (= CMP J1.21 + J1.22); MRuiz
66.1−7; Nahón 24; Pinto 2; PTJ 54*c* (= Alvar).
//Beutler 13; Braga, I, 263−276; FM 12; RPM 35−46; VRP 235−248.
///ASW 455; H. A. Rennert, "Lieder des Juan Rodríguez del Padrón," *ZRPh*,
17 (1893), 544−558: p. 549, manuscript version, vv. 19−32 (¡Quién tuviese
atal ventura / con sus amores folgare!); Luis Vélez de Guevara, *El conde don
Sancho Niño*, ed. Roberto J. Bininger and Ricardo L. Landeira (Vigo: "Faro de
Vigo," 1970), pp. 23−26, 123−124 (Levántase el Conde Niño, / la mañana de
San Juan).
////For possible distant European congeners (*La Pernette*; *Les Métamorphoses*;
The Twa Magicians; *Amore inevitabile*; *Søster beder Broder*; and others), see
Yoná, pp. 157−165, 172−173; Samuel G. Armistead, Raúl Barrientos, and
Judith Büki, "Tres baladas húngaras y sus vínculos con el Romancero his-
pánico," *CuH*, 371 (May 1981), 313−319.

24. *Diego León (á-a) (Diego León)* (MP 63/J5) (**Tangier**): Young Diego León
(Griego León, Žuego León) grows up in Toledo and Granada. He falls in love
with and courts Doña Juana, daughter of a rich family. He asks her father, Don
Pedro, for her hand in marriage, but he rebuffs León, because of his lack of
money and Doña Juana's youth. Don Pedro mocks León. The daughter begs to
be allowed to marry him, but Don Pedro, recognizing her love for León, locks
her in a room so León cannot see her. He hires four thugs to kill the young man,
but the latter kills three of them and wounds the other (or: He kills some,
wounds others, and throws others into the water). Having lost his weapons,
León hurls himself into the sea, but returns for Juana three days later. He throws
three pebbles up at her window. She does not answer immediately and he
begins to doubt she still loves him, but she rushes down stairs "like a wild
lioness" and into his arms. They are married the next day.
    Benardete's version is no exception to the general uniformity of the Moroc-
can tradition of *Diego León*. V. 35 is, however, worthy of note. It is a
contamination from a rare *romance vulgar: El mal casamiento impedido (á-a)*.
See CMP S19, T4.4; Ortega, pp. 217−218 (vv. 19−32); PTJ 118.19−32.

Bibliography:

/ASK 63(20); Bénichou 269; Bennaim MS 73; Boas–Nahón 4; Castro MS 23; CMP J5.1–11; Essayag MS 6–10; Fereres MS 1; Fernández, pp. 315–317; FRS 41; Gallent 5; Larrea 82–84; Levy, II, 30; IV, 6; Librowicz 13; Librowicz (II) J5; Librowicz, "Gibraltar," no. 6; MP 63 (= CMP J5.11); MRuiz 70; Nahón 26*A*–26*B*; PTJ 63*A*; Pulido, p. 54 (= MP); Thomas, p. 291 (= Bénichou).

//CVR 56; FM 104; RQDB-I, 35.

///Samuel G. Armistead and Joseph H. Silverman, "Sobre el romance 'En vna Villa pequeña' (*Xácaras y romances varios*, Málaga, 1668)," *Sef*, 31 (1971), 184–186 (En vna Villa pequeña, / la qual llaman de la Algava).

25. *La amante abandonada* (polyas.) (*The Abandoned Mistress*) (K2) (**Salonika**): This tantalizingly ambiguous ballad is open to a variety of interpretations. We are faced immediately with an unidentified individual who is intensely enamored of a woman he cannot forget and whom he visits in the early mornings and afternoons. On the occasions he finds her still asleep, he covers her and leaves. But when she is awake, he kisses and embraces her and chats with her. She begins to weep. He asks her why: Is she afraid of something, is she newly with child or suffering the pain of unrequited love? She explains to her interlocutor—now identified as a king—that she was brought up in Seville among honorable people. A knight named Andarleto (Andarneto) fell in love with her. He slept with her for three nights, nights that to her (to him?) seemed like three weeks. She (he?) prepared a golden ladder for him beneath her window, so that he might come and go as if he were at home. But, after those three nights, he left her for another love.

Perhaps it is the king himself who visits her with such tender love, so solicitous of her well-being. He does call her *cativada*, thus suggesting that she may be a prisoner in his care. Elsewhere we have written: "It is as if the girl were some captive Christian in a *novela morisca*, relating to her noble Arabic master, already enamored of her singular beauty and grace, the intimate details of her short-lived relationship with a donjuanesque knight of irresistible charms" (*Yoná*, p. 194). The text includes an interesting use of the "euphemistic third person" (v. 11*a*) in order to separate the young speaker from the events of the illicit love affair that she is describing. We are now preparing a detailed study of the ballad and its relationship to *La mujer engañada* and a number of popular lyric songs.

Bibliography: Amiras MS 31 vo.; ASK 74(2); Attias 43; CMP K2.1–8; Crews MS 24.1–16; FRS 43 (= LRI); LSO, p. 92; Mano, p. 46 (= GRI); Onís 3; *Yoná* 15.

26. *El pájaro verde (á-a) (The Green Bird)* (MP 66/K5) (**Tangier**): A beautiful young lady grows up in Madrid. Her family wants to arrange a marriage of financial convenience with her uncle, even though she is in love with her young neighbor. The two lovers plan to elope, but her relatives find the young man working in the fields and stab him to death. When the girl hears death bells tolling, she goes to her room, tearing her hair with grief. Before the confessor arrives, she dies of a broken heart (or she wraps herself in a white sheet and stabs herself to death). They open the door and find only a "green bird singing to the sound of the water." The two lovers are buried side by side and flowers (rose or lily and carnation) grow from their graves.

Bibliography:
/ASK 66(6); Bennaim MS 77; CMP K5.1–6; Essayag MS 30–32; Larrea 86–89; MP 66 (= CMP K5.1); MRuiz 73; PTJ 65.
//Braga, I, 615–619.

27. *El conde Alarcos (í-a) (Count Alarcos)* (MP 64/L1) (**Salonika**): The unhappy princess complains to the king that he has not yet found a husband for her: Fifteen-year-old girls already have husbands and children and she, who is twenty-four, is still unmarried. Yet she is not without a rich dowry and good fortune. Her father replies that it is her own fault. She could have been the wife of the Count of Seville, who is now married and has children.

Most published texts, both from the East and from Morocco, are fragmentary. The Menéndez Pidal collection includes more extensive, unedited Moroccan versions collected at the turn of the century (CMP L1). The Eastern form is exclusively Salonikan (or from nearby towns: Karaferia, Larissa). Most versions are very short and are contaminated, after Benardete's v. 6, with *La fuente fecundante (í-a)* (CMP R5). Benardete's version is an exception in that it is uncontaminated and in v. 7 takes the narrative one stage further than any other published text.

Bibliography: ASK 64(7); Attias 23; CMP L1.1–10; Crews MS 25; Haboucha 3; Hemsi 19.1–8; Onís 7; PTJ 64 (= Hemsi).
/Alvar, *Cantos*, p. 335; ASK 64(3); Benarroch, p. 87; CMP L1.11–25; Larrea 85; Librowicz (II) L1; MP 64; MRuiz 72; Nahón 25.11–17, 27; PTJ 64*a*–64*b* (= MRuiz, Alvar).

//AFC 3029; Braga, I, 483–556; FM 6; Milá 237; RPM 134; VRP 130–182, 1001, 1022.
///*Primav*. 163 (Retraída está la infanta, / bien así como solía).
////Nigra 8 (*La figlia del re*). Note the detailed study by Luciano García Lorenzo, *El tema del conde Alarcos: Del Romancero a Jacinto Grau* (Madrid: C.S.I.C., 1972). See also Samuel G. Armistead, Iacob M. Hassán, and Joseph H. Silverman, "Four Moroccan Judeo-Spanish Folksong *Incipits* (1824–1825)," *HR*, 42 (1974), 83–87.

28. *La mala suegra (á-e) (The Evil Mother-in-Law)* (MP 70/L4) (28*A*: **Salonika**; 28*B*: **Çanakkale**): The queen (Miraibella, Mirabella, Amiralibelya, Amiralbelya), feeling birth pangs, wishes she could give birth at her parents' palace. Her mother-in-law overhears what she is saying and affectionately tells her to go, promising to prepare food for her husband and for his horse (mule) and hawk during her absence and to give bones to the dog so it will not follow her. The queen departs and, as she arrives at her parents' house, gives birth to a beautiful baby boy (with a golden arrow in his hand and a diamond star). Her husband returns and, when he asks for his wife, is informed by the mother-in-law that she has gone off, after cursing them both, threatening her with a stick, and calling her an old whore and him the son of an evil father. Furious, the king rushes off, swearing (on his sword) to kill his wife. Along the way, he meets messengers, who tell him his son has been born. The king curses mother and son. He arrives at the house of his parents-in-law and accuses and threatens his wife. She swears it is not true and convinces him of her innocence (or the newborn child speaks miraculously to prove his mother's innocence). The king swears (on his crown, his sword) to return home and kill his mother. He kills her.

Text 28*A* consists of an assemblage of proverbial expressions. According to Benardete, the informant knew a full version of the ballad identical to Coello 12, but added these proverbial verses at the end. Verse 1 is a traditional formula, used for introducing proverbs or set phrases, which occurs in other *romances* as well: "Así oyí yo decir, / en ca de mi padre señor" (*Vos labraré un pendón*: Nahón 61); "Siempre oí decir . . ." (Larrea 183). For other literary examples, compare: "Siempre, Sancho, lo he oído decir, que el hacer bien a villanos es echar agua en el mar" (*Don Quijote*, ed. Américo Castro [Mexico City: Porrúa, 1960], p. 102*a* [I, 23]), see also p. 385*b* (II, 32); " . . . siempre oí decir que las cosas de amor avivan el ingenio" (Francisco Delicado, *La lozana andaluza*, ed. Bruno M. Damiani [Madrid: Castalia,

1972], p. 162; other examples: pp. 168, 174 [= Mamotretos 38, 40, 42]); "Siempre lo oy dezir, que es más difícile de sofrir la próspera fortuna que la aduersa" (Fernando de Rojas, *La Celestina* [Madrid: "Clásicos Castellanos," 1954], II, 71 [Act 11]); "De gustos siempre oí dezir que no ha de disputar" (Baltasar Gracián, *El Criticón*, ed. M. Romera-Navarro [Philadelphia: University of Pennsylvania Press, 1940], III, 285). This same phrase occurs at the end of Moroccan versions of *La mala suegra*:

> Siempre la oí decir,   en la casa de mi padre,
> que las suegras y las nueras   siempre se quieren male.
> (Ortega 224; Larrea 96.47)

For other examples and references, see *Yoná*, p. 232, n. 10.

To Benardete's v. 2, we find no exact counterpart in Sephardic proverb collections. Note the use of a similar expression in *Diego León*: "Que los bienes de este mundo, / Dios los daba y los quitaba"(Nahón 26A.21). Spanish *refraneros* offer various similar sayings:

> Bienes de fortuna, mudables como luna.
> Bienes de este mundo, sombra o humo.
> Bienes y males son ambulantes: hoy están aquí y mañana en
>   otra parte.

(Francisco Rodríguez Marín, *Más de 21.000 refranes castellanos . . .* [Madrid: RABM, 1926], p. 56; idem, *Los 6.666 refranes . . .* [Madrid: C. Bermejo, 1934], p. 31; idem, *Todavía 10.700 refranes más . . .* [Madrid: Prensa Española, 1941], p. 44).

V. 3 is not itself proverbial. It occurs in both Sephardic and Peninsular versions of *La mala suegra* and is, of course, essential to the ballad:

> que la esjuegra con la almuera   siempre se quisieron male.
> (Díaz Plaja 3)
> que las suegras y las nueras   siempre se quisieron mal.
> (RPM 150, 141, 147; RTR 9)

Adatto's version of *La mala suegra* (15a)includes what would seem to be an authentic proverb, which, however, we have not found in any of the Sephardic

collections consulted: "Y la esuegra con la hermuera / es la šufre con la tea."
The sentiment expressed is, of course, altogether characteristic of the *refranes*.
See Luis Martínez Kleiser, *Refranero general ideológico español* (Madrid:
Real Academia Española, 1953), pp. 675−676. See also *Yoná*, pp. 176−177.

Vv. 4−5 constitute a well-known proverb: "El suegro y el yerno: como sol
de invierno. Sale tadre y se va presto" (Enrique Saporta y Beja, *Refranero
sefardí* [Madrid and Barcelona: C.S.I.C., 1957], p. 284; H. V. Besso,
"Judeo-Spanish Proverbs," *BHi*, 50 [1948], 370−387: no. 72; idem, "A
Further Contribution to the Refranero judeo-español," *BHi*, 37 [1935], 209−
219: no. 49). A similar saying is applied to the mother-in-law (Saporta, p. 284;
Abraham Galante, "Proverbes judéo-espagnols," *BHi*, 9 [1902], 440−454:
no. 197).

V. 6 is also proverbial: "La madre con la ija como la unia con la carne"
(David Elnecave, "Folklore de los sefardíes de Turquía," offprint from *Sef*, 23
[1963], part IV, no. 160). For abundant additional documentation, see our
article, "El cancionero judeo-español de Marruecos en el siglo XVIII (*Incipits
de los Ben-Çûr*)," *NRFH*, 22 (1973), 280−290: p. 287, n. 13; also CMP
O1.7; *Yoná*, p. 176.

V. 7 is the proverb: "El padre con el fijo: como la piedra con el anillo"
(Saporta, p. 230; Galante, "Proverbes," no. 114; Besso "Judeo-Spanish
Proverbs," no. 68; idem, "A Further Contribution," no. 46). For similar
proverbial endings to *La mala suegra*, compare CMP L4.4, 5, 7, 13; Díaz-
Plaja 3; Hemsi 43.

Vv. 22−26 of version 28*B*, with the wife's mother's curse against the
husband's mother, the death of "the queen" (?) and the wife's oath turned into
a blessing of the newborn child, reflect a clumsy effort on the part of the
informant to bring an incomplete version to some sort of satisfactory close.

Bibliography: Adatto 15*a*−15*b*; Adatto MS 9−11; ASK 70 (23); Attias 38;
Benmayor 29*a*−29*d*; Coello 12; CMP L4.1−17; Danon 9; Díaz-Plaja 3;
DRH 7 (= TCR A7); Gil 27 (= Coello, Danon); Hemsi 43; Levy, III, 8; IV,
11; MP 70 (= Coello); MPelayo 13 (= Danon); Onís 20; PTJ 69 (= Díaz-
Plaja); SBS 16; SICh 5 (= TCR B5); TCR A7, B5 (= DRH, SICh); *Yoná* 14.
/ASK 70 (8); Castro MS 45; CMP L4.18−24; Larrea 94−96; Librowicz (II)
L4; MP 70, 2d text (= CMP L4.18); MRuiz 54; Ortega 224; PTJ 69*a*
(= Ortega). See also Benoliel, "Hakitía," XIV, 225.

//AFC 2326; Braga, I, 556−572, 577−582, 584−590; Milá 243; RPM 135−155; VRP 554−578. See also *Yoná* 14.

29. *La malcasada del pastor* (*ó*) + *Juan Lorenzo* (*á*) (*The Shepherd's Mismated Wife* + *Juan Lorenzo*) (MP 72 / L8 + MP 12 / C2) (**Tetuán** [or **Tangier**?]): The Moroccan form of *La malcasada del pastor* embodies the following narrative: A young girl, whose father is from France, but whose mother is not, is married by her parents (father, mother) to the best (the worst; the greatest) among all the shepherds (to a gentleman). He beats and mistreats her. He sits at table and eats meat, fish, and white bread, drinks soup and wine, and sleeps on a pillow in a bed; she sits on the floor and is given bones, black (brown, bran) bread, broth, and water, and sleeps on the floor with her own arm as a pillow. [To test her fidelity], her husband sends her at midnight (or before dawn) on a tiring walk to a distant fountain to fetch water. The running water lulls her to sleep beside the fountain (or: As she is filling the jug, she falls asleep). A knight (or page) passes by and gives her one (three, four, five, seven) kiss(es). The girl wakes up and tells the knight (or page) that she is married. If her husband finds out, he will leave (kill) her. The man tells her that he is her husband and carries her home: "Now I am your honored wife." They live happily. "Good always comes of waiting."

We find no documentation for the proverbial ending: "Todo el que espera /a bien allega" (RLH, IX, no. IV.36, p. 317). Compare, however: "Quen espera, come la pera" (D. Elnecavé, "Folklore de los sefardíes de Turquía," offprint from *Sef*, 23 [1963], 204 [no. 284]); "Cuanto más está la pera en el peral, más espera su buen mazal" (Denah Lida, "Refranes judeo-españoles de Esmirna," *NRFH*, 12 [1958], 1−35: no. 48).

For the **Bibliography** of *La malcasada del pastor*, see no. 15 *supra*.

The Moroccan versions of *Juan Lorenzo* tell the following story: A marvelous (white) ship, with deck boards of coral (fine walnut), sails of rich cloth (silk), and rigging of gold (twisted silk thread), is seen approaching over the sea; all its passengers are of royal blood and the King of Portugal and all his followers (and Juan Lorenzo) are on board. Some say it is coming for war and others that it is coming in peace. Juan Lorenzo (Žuan Lorenso) has a banquet of chickens, capons, and pigeons and white and red wine prepared. During the banquet, the king proclaims that all his subjects' beautiful wives must parade before him; anyone whose wife does not appear will be called a cuckold (or coward; or: whoever does not appear willingly will be dragged out with ropes).

Only Juan Lorenzo's wife appears. The king takes her by the hand and leads her into a garden, praising her beauty above that of all other women. He plucks a rose and gives it to her. He threatens to have Juan Lorenzo killed; the wife asks that he be exiled instead. The king lies down in her lap so she can delouse him. She slits his throat and after three days (the next morning), Juan Lorenzo reigns in his stead.

For **Bibliography**, see no. 6 *supra*.

30. *La mujer engañada* (*í-a*) (*The Deceived Wife*) (MP 74 / L13) (**Izmir**): A young man marries a girl from a rich family. After nine months, she bears him a child. After ten months, he falls in love with someone else. He leaves his wife at home and goes to work in the fields, but the wife follows him and sees him go into the house of a beautiful girl. The abandoned wife enters and sees fine food and her husband flirting with the girl. (The husband is toasting the girl with a glass of wine and expressing the wish that they have a child.) The wife goes further into the house and sees beds with fine curtains prepared and the pair in their underclothes. (The girl is wearing the wife's jewels.) She sadly returns home, locks her door with seven bolts and consoles herself by singing a lullaby to her infant daughter concerning what she has seen. Her husband returns at midnight and asks to be admitted, saying he is tired from working in his vineyards. She tells him he has been with the other girl. The husband offers her bracelets, but she tells him to return to where he came from and remain there until the next day; and that the girl is not more beautiful than she is. Unwillingly, she goes to the rabbi the next morning and asks him to dissolve her marriage.

Bibliography: Adatto MS, pp. 16–18; ASK 74 (18); Attias 43.33–61; Bassan 153; Benmayor 30*a*–30*b*; *Bosnia* C11; CMP L13.1–12; Crews MS 24, XII; Danon 32; Estrugo, *Los sefardíes*, p. 137; idem, "Reminiscencias," p. 75; idem, "Tradiciones españolas," p. 145; Gil 41 (= Danon); Haboucha 4; Hemsi 44; Hollander 14*A*–14*D*; Levy, I, 19; III, 135; IV, 29, 75; LSO, p. 70 (no. 1.27–33); Manrique de Lara, *Blanco y Negro*, texts 3 and 4; Mendoza, *El romance español y el corrido mexicano*, p. 37 (= Manrique de Lara); Milner–Storm 45 (= Levy, I, 19); Milwitzky MS 37, 51; MPelayo 43 (= Danon); Onís 29; PTJ 73 (= Danon); SBS 97; Simoni 3; SRC BR24 (= Danon).
/ASK 74(19); Bénichou 129; Boas–Nahón 5; Castro MS 13; CMP L13.13–23; Fereres MS 15; Gil 41 (= MP); Larrea 103–106; Librowicz 14;

Librowicz (II) L13; Librowicz, "Gibraltar," no. 8; MP 74 (= MP L13.13); MRuiz 57; Nahón 32*A*−32*B*; Ortega 221; PTJ 73*a* (= Bénichou); Torner, *Lírica hispánica*, no. 145 (p. 245). Note the eighteenth-century Moroccan *incipit*: "Pénsase biyyano / ke me adormesí'a" (Armistead−Silverman, "*Incipits* de los Ben Çûr," p. 288, no. 12).
//Braga, II, 276−277; FM 50; Milá 408; RPM 298. For more Bibliography, see *Yoná*, p. 195.
///Alonso−Blecua 208; *Yoná*, p. 195 (Pensóse el villano / que me adormecía).

31. *El rapto (í-a) (The Abduction)* (MP 94/O5) (**Tangier**): The count greets the beautiful Blancaniña and declares himself a prisoner of his love for her; her beauty proves fatal to the men of the town. The girl rejects him, saying that, if her father finds out, he will be furious, but the count seizes her in his arms and carries her off to the sea, where his boat awaits them. They embark. The girl weeps. He consoles her: He is not carrying her off as a captive; she will be mistress of a hundred and twenty cities and as many palaces, and queen of Andalusia. He will remove her parents and brothers from their menial livelihoods and give them important positions. The girl is comforted. The wedding is celebrated the next day.

Vv. 1*b* and 6*b* of Benardete's text are corrupt. The grotesque "que en todas mis gansas" (1*b*) must originally have read "que en toda Vizcaya" (as against "que en toda Vitoria" in Lope's text). The Castro MS conserves a distorted vestige of this reading: "que en toda bidkana" (p. 29). Other modern versions offer a *lectio facilior*: "que en toda España" (Larrea 141; Ortega). The senseless "por Dios, Catuliña" (v. 6*b*) was once "por Dios, que a ti riña," attested, with variations, in several other modern texts:

> por Dios, que a ti riña (Larrea 141.12)
> por Dios, que arméis riña (MP 94.5*b*)
> por Dios, que a mí riña (Nahón 41.4*b*)

Ortega's "por Dios, cati riña" gives us the first step toward the meaningless reading of Benardete's version. Compare, in Lope's text: "Si me ve mi madre, / a fe que me riña" (Alonso).

Bibliography:
/ASK 94 (1); Bénichou 147; Castro MS 29; CMP O5.1−6; Larrea 140−141; MP 94 (= MP O5.2); Nahón 41; Ortega 226; PTJ 94 (= Ortega).

///Bénichou, pp. 325–326 (Reverencia os hago / linda vizcaína). The poem is from *Los prados de León* by Lope de Vega. See also Dámaso Alonso, *Poesía de la Edad Media y poesía de tipo tradicional* (Buenos Aires: Losada, 1942), pp. 379–380.

32. *El forzador* (*í-a*) (*The Abductor*) (MP 96/O7) (**Salonika**): Ladies and maidens appear at a window. A richly dressed knight passes by and his horse stops, dazzled by the beauty of the maidens. The knight looks up and falls in love with the youngest. He promises her all his riches, but she rejects him, alleging the greater wealth of her father, the Count (Duke, a grandee) of Seville (or threatening to have the knight dragged). On being rejected, the knight asks where the girl lives and she answers in the high towers of Seville. He determines to go there and completes a fifteen-day journey in seven (eight) days. At midnight, he knocks at her door. He finds everything closed and forces his way in (with his fist; with magic words). Once inside the house, he becomes confused and cannot find his way. He finds the girl asleep among flowers and puts his hand (his fist, a knife) on her breast (or speaks words of love to her). The girl wakes up (or does not wake up). She is frightened and asks who he is. She threatens to utter a scream that will bring all Seville to her aid. (She warns him she is betrothed to the duke of France.) The knight flees, cursing all women (or threatens to kill her parents and all Seville with his sword and she agrees to go with him; or he throws her over his shoulder and carries her off to Sicily on his horse).

Bibliography: Armistead–Silverman, "Arabic Refrains," p. 94; ASK 96(8); Attias 52; CBU, pp. 338–339 (= UR); CMP O7.1–12; Crews MS 30; DRH 3*a*–3*b* (= TCR A3*a*–3*b*); FRS 57; LSO, pp. 71–72, 89; PTJ 97–97*a* (= DRH, UR); SICh 2 (= TCR B2); TCR A3*a*–3*b*, B2 (= DRH, SICh); UR, 9, p. 373 (= CBU, pp. 338–339); *Yoná* 19.
/ASK 96(6); Bénichou 244; Bennaim MS 10; Castro MS 12; CMP O6.1–8; Larrea 144–145; Librowicz (II) O6; MP 96 (= O6.1 + O6.2); MRuiz 79; PTJ 96 (= Bénichou).
//Braga, I, 590–593, 594–596; CVR 42; VRP 464–477. For more Peninsular versions, see TCR A3; *Yoná*, p. 266.
////See *Yoná*, p. 266.

33. *Silvana* (*í-a*) (*Silvana*) (MP 98/P1) (**Salonika**): Silvana is strolling through her garden (room; yard), playing a golden guitar (a golden flute) and singing

ballads. Her father, the king, hears her and falls in love with her, saying she is more beautiful in her everyday clothes than is the queen, her mother, dressed in fine clothing. He asks her to be his mistress. Silvana asks who will suffer the torments of Hell for her. Her father says that he will suffer them. She protests that she must bathe first and goes off crying to heaven for justice. Her mother, the queen, hears her cries and asks what is troubling her. After the queen reassures her, they exchange dresses and the queen instructs Silvana to tell the king not to light candles that night. The queen, in Silvana's stead, goes to sleep with the king, thus saving him from sin.

Bibliography: Adatto MS, pp. 30–31; Adatto Recordings 14, 25; ASK 98(5); Attias 41; Baruch, pp. 286–287; *Bosnia* A3, B16 (B16 = Baruch); CMP P1.1–17, P1.24; Crews MS 13; FRS 58*A*; Levy, I, 2; Onís 39; PTJ 98 (= Baruch); UYA, pp. 172–175; *Yoná* 20.
/ASK 98(2); CMP P1.18–23; FRS 58*B*; Larrea 147; MP 98 (= CMP P1.18).
//Beutler 14 (nos. 114–121); FM 21; Milá 272; RPM 162. See also *Yoná*, pp. 271–272, for more bibliography.
///Francisco Manuel de Mello, *Auto do Fidalgo Aprendiz* (Lisbon: Domingos Carneiro, 1676), ed. José V. de Pina Martins (Lisbon: O Mundo do Livro, 1966), p. 11 (Passeavase Silvana / por hum corredor hum dia). The work was composed in 1646. See RVP, pp. 142–143; RoH, I, 160; II, 408, n. 5; *Yoná*, p. 273. The Eastern *incipit*, "Paseábase Silvana," can be documented in 1587, 1599, 1618, 1628 and 1753 (Avenary, "Cantos," no. 147). The first extensive Judeo-Spanish text dates from the eighteenth century: *Bosnia* A3.

34. *Delgadina* (*á-a*) (*Delgadina*) (MP 99/P2) (**Salonika**): A king (of France) has three beautiful daughters. One is called Oro (or Fatme); the other, Plata (or Xerifé); the youngest is called Delgadina (Delgadilla; Delgadica; Delgazina; Delguezina; Delgazía; Dalguezía; Delgadino; Delgadiña; Delgadía; Elgazina). One day, while they are seated at table (or at mass), her father stares at her. The girl asks him why he is looking at her. He wants her to be his mistress. The girl rejects him. The father calls his knights (pages; Moors; servants) and orders them to lock her in a tower (hut; castle; high building; palaces; galleys; chains; prison; box) and give her salted (burnt; raw; ram's; donkey's) meat (and dry bread) to eat and bitter orange or pomegranate juice (bitter water) to drink. After a certain time (eight, fifteen days; three, four weeks; thirty days), the girl looks out the window (her relatives visit her) and she asks her brothers, sisters, mother, and father consecutively to give her a glass of water, for she is dying of

thirst. They refuse. Finally her father (mother) brings (or orders the servants to bring) her water (and well-cooked meat). At that moment (or: as she is drinking the water), Delgadina expires. (Her father orders the punishment to be repeated and the girl dies.)

Bibliography: Adatto 11; Adatto MS, pp. 32–34; Adatto Recordings 12, 23; ASK 99(8); Attias 45; Benmayor 18*a*–18*c*; *Bosnia* C15; Cohen, pp. 38, 54; CMP P2.1–15, P2.28; Danon 14; Díaz–Plaja 7; Elnecavé 5; FRS 59*A*; Gil 54 (= Danon); Granell, pp. 291–292 (= Díaz–Plaja, with minor variations); Hemsi 9; Hemsi, "Evocation," p. 1059; Hollander 18; JG(Add.) 8; Lazar, p. 43 (= Danon); Levy, II, 27–28; IV, 7; Milner–Storm 5 (= Levy, II, 27); Milwitzky MS 11; Milwitzky, "Viajero," pp. 326–327 (= Milwitzky MS 11); MP 99 (= Danon); MPelayo 26 (= Danon); Noga Alberti, *Comunidades*, pp. 264–265; Onís 10; Pla 1 (= Hemsi); PTJ 99 (= Danon); SBS 47–49.
/ASK 99(9); Bénichou 252; CMP P2.16–27; FRS 59*B*; Larrea 148–149, 161; Librowicz 20; Librowicz (II) P2; Librowicz, "Gibraltar," no. 9; MRuiz 80; Nahón 42; Ortega 234; PTJ 99*a* (= Ortega); Rechnitz 2.
//AFC 2382; Beutler 15; Braga, I, 451–455, 469–473; FM 22; Milá 29; RPM 163–174; VRP 479–514. See also *Yoná*, p. 272, for more bibliography.
///The Eastern *incipits* "Estábase la Delgadita" and "Delgadina, Delgadina" date from 1555 and 1684–1753 respectively (Avenary, "Cantos," no. 78 and 48).

35. *Gerineldo* (*í-o*) (*Gerineldo*) (MP 101/Q1) (**Tangier**): Who might have the good fortune of Gerineldo (Žirineldo, Girilendo, Žirinendo, Girinerdo) "to gain what has been lost!" On Sunday morning, Gerineldo is cleaning (cutting) silk cloths for the king. The princess (queen) calls to the king's (queen's; princess') page (valet; knight), Gerineldo: She would like him to spend three hours with her in her castle. Gerineldo answers that, since he is her servant, she must be joking with him. She answers that she is speaking seriously. Gerineldo asks when he should come. He should come at midnight (at 11:30; between 12:00 and 1:00; at first cock crowing), when the king (sultan) is asleep; he should wear woolen (canvas, silk, soft) shoes, so no one will hear him. Twelve (and one) o'clock comes and Gerineldo has not arrived. The princess cries out against him. At that moment, Gerineldo arrives. He knocks at the door of the castle. She asks who this daring thief is who is knocking at such an hour. It is Gerineldo, who is coming "for what has been promised." She throws down a

golden ladder and he climbs up (or she goes down in her petticoat to open the door for him). He finds a luxurious bed has been made up for him. After making love, they both fall asleep. The king wakes up, finds the ladder and climbs up. He finds them asleep "like man and wife" ("like brother and sister") and wonders if he should kill them both, but decides to say nothing and to place his (golden) sword (dagger) between them. The princess, "feeling the cold sword," wakes up and arouses Gerineldo, saying there is no hope for them. Gerineldo asks where he should go; she answers that he should go out into the garden (thickets). Gerineldo leaves very sadly, sighing as he goes down the stairs. On the last step (or as he goes out the door of the castle or along the way), he meets the king, who says he looks pale (sad; pensive) and asks where he has been. He answers that he has been in the king's garden, "picking roses and lilies." The fragrance of a rose (a flower) has confused him (made him pallid). The king accuses him of sleeping with the princess. Gerineldo says that it is his fault and asks the king to kill him. The king will not kill him; tomorrow he will marry the princess. Gerineldo answers that he has sworn by the Virgin of the Star (or on "the book of the star"; on his prayer book; to his aged parents) not to marry any woman whom he has slept with (or he marries the princess the next day).

Vv. 28−29 of Benardete's text occur in most Moroccan versions of *Gerineldo*. They are a contamination from *Sufrir callando*. Cf. Larrea 97.21−24, 98.23−28; MP 71; CMP L7; Milá 252.9−11.

Bibliography: Attias 21; CMP Q1.1−2; Vol. III, 42−43; Luria MS 2; PTJ 101 (= Attias).
/Alvar, "Gerineldo," pp. 128−132 (Alcazarquivir = MRuiz); idem, *Romancero: Tradicionalidad*, p. 402 (= PTJ 101*b*); ASK 101(23); Bénichou 81; Bennaim MS 60; Boas−Nahón 7*A*-7*B*; Castro MS 39; CMP Q1.3−12; Fereres MS 12−13; Larrea 151−156; Librowicz 21; Librowicz (II) Q1; MP 101 (= CMP Q1.3); MRuiz 82; Nahón 43*A*−43*B*; Pinto 9, 11; PTJ 101*a*-101*b* (= Alvar, "Gerineldo," pp. 128−130: Tetuán *A*, Larache *A*). All known Sephardic versions of *Gerineldo* collected up to the date of publication are brought together in RLH, VI-VIII: Moroccan texts: nos. I.475−508 (also I.506 *bis* [Vol. VIII, 367]) and II.1-16 *bis* (the latter series joined to *El conde Sol*; and, in some cases, to *El prisionero* + *Conde Niño*); Eastern texts: I.511−513. Note also the synthetic version published in Ramon Menéndez Pidal, Diego Catalán, and Alvaro Galmés, *Cómo vive un romance: Dos ensayos sobre tradicionalidad* (Madrid: *RFE*, Anejo LX, 1954), p. 198f. As the editors of RLH point out, the fragment published by Estrugo, "Reminiscencias," p. 72,

and *Los sefardíes*, p. 129, is not from Judeo-Spanish tradition. See no. I.510.
// AFC 2325; Beutler 12; Braga, I, 177–206; FM 7; Milá 269; RPM 65–81;
VRP 257–274, 1004. See RLH, Vols. VI, VII, VIII.
///*Primav*. 161–161a (Levantóse Gerineldo / que al rey dejara dormido;
Gerineldo, Gerineldo, / el mi paje más querido).
////Cf. DVM, II, núm. 62 *(Der Spielmannssohn)* and CMP Q1.

36. *Repulsa y compasión (á) (Rejection and Compassion)* (MP 115/S5)
(**Tetuán**): A girl gets up before dawn and goes to the seaside to fill her water
pitcher (or with a basin to bathe). She meets a dark-haired young man (a page; a
gentleman), who tries to deceive her. She pushes him into the sea, but then
takes pity on him, throws her tresses down to him, pulls him out of the water,
takes him to her house, and prepares a bed of roses covered with lemon leaves
and a pillow of orange blossoms for him.

    Bibliography: Attias, "Çẽrôr," no. 8; CMP S5.1 (= Attias, "Çẽrôr").
/ ASK 115(3); CMP S5.2–3; Larrea 169–171; Librowicz 22; Librowicz (II)
S5; Milner–Storm 14 (= Larrea 170); MP 115 (= CMP S5.2); MRuiz 89.

37. *El sueño de la hija* (polyas.) *(The Daughter's Dream)* (MP 68; 129/S6)
(**Izmir**): The King (Queen) of France has three daughters (or: Fire destroys all
of Istanbul except for one little house where three sisters live): One is embroidering (or cutting [cloth]); the other, sewing; the youngest is embroidering on a
frame. The youngest falls asleep. Her mother is furious and wants to beat her
(wakes her). The daughter begs her not to strike her; she has dreamed a
symbolic dream with a happy meaning: (The King of France wants her "as his
friend.") Her mother interprets the dream: The golden pillar (golden pine tree,
rosary, rope, cord, cooking pan) beside the well is her bridegroom (husband),
the king (king's son); the three (seven) golden birds are her brothers-in-law (her
children; stepchildren; servants); the full moon at (behind) the door is her
mother-in-law (father-in-law), the queen (king); the (golden) apple (lemon)
tree (the sun) by the mirror (closet; in the garden) is her father-in-law, the king;
the basil plant is the king and the people; the morning star at the window is her
sister-in-law (mother-in-law), the queen; the seven (twelve) stars are her
sisters-in-law (relatives; maids); the three apples are her sisters; the nightingale
is her brother-in-law's son. At that moment, carriages appear at the door to
carry her off to a foreign land. Messengers have come from the King (of Spain)
to ask the hand of the youngest daughter in marriage.

El sueño de la hija is one of a number of Sephardic *romances* which are translations of Greek ballads. See Armistead—Silverman, "A New Collection," pp. 138—139 (no. 7). Cf. also no. 38 *infra*. Hollander has studied the Sephardic ballad in detail (pp. 205—214).

Bibliography: Adatto MS 7—8; Adatto Recordings 10; ASK 68(27); Attias 60; Baruch, p. 288; Benmayor 37*a*—37*d*; Besso, "Los sefardíes y el idioma," p. 189; *Bosnia* B19 (= Baruch); Cantera Ortiz, p. 27 (= San Sebastián); Cohen, p. 57; CMP S6.1—13, 18; Crews MS 11; Danon 5; Estrugo, *Los sefardíes*, p. 127; FRS 64; Gil 17 (= Danon); Hemsi 16; Hemsi, "Evocation," p. 1056 (II) (= Hemsi); Hollander 21*A*—21*E*; Katz, "Ladino Literature"; Levy, II, 24—25; IV, 9; LSO, pp. 74—75; Milwitzky MS 30, 61; MP 69 (= Danon); MPelayo 17 (= Danon); Moya, II, 257; Onís 40; PTJ 67 (= Danon); San Sebastián 8 (= Danon + v. 5); SBS 53.

/ASK 129(4); Castro MS 34; CMP S6.14—17; Larrea 197; Librowicz 23; Librowicz (II) S6; Librowicz, "Gibraltar," no. 14; MP 129 (= S6.14); MRuiz 52; PTJ 67*a*.

///A two-verse citation, "Aquel rey de Francia / tres hijas tenía // la una labraba / la otra cosía," appears in a Hebrew hymnal dating from 1702 (Attias, *Cancionero*, p. 363, no. 4).

////Abbott, *Songs of Modern Greece*, pp. 112—113; Frye, *The Marble Threshing Floor*, no. 56 and p. 292 (*Tò óneiron tēs kórēs / The Girl's Dream*).

38. *El pozo airón* (*ó*) (*The Bottomless Well*) (X13) (**Salonika**): Seven brothers depart for Aragón (Lahor). Along the way, their water gives out. The heat is intense and they don't find water. They keep on their way and find a deep well (*pogo airón*). They cast lots and the lot falls to the youngest. They tie him to a rope and drop him into the well, but the rope breaks. The water turns into blood and the stones of the well are like snakes and scorpions eating out his heart. Embittered, the six brothers start to turn back. From the well, the young man calls out to them: They should tell his mother that he remained behind (or that she has been deprived of her youngest son); his father, that he is in the well (or that he has been deprived of his son); his wife, that she has just become a widow; and his children, that they have just become orphans.

El pozo airón is a close translation of the Greek ballad *Tò stoicheiōméno pēgádi*. See NSR, pp. 75, n. 65, 78. The Judeo-Spanish song is a dirge traditionally sung during *Tišʿa bĕ-Āb* (the nine days of mourning, during August, for the destruction of the Temple).

Bibliography: ASK 143c(2); Attias 83; Bassan 15; CMP X13.1−3; Levy, *Antología*, IV, nos. 210−211 (pp. 325−327); LSO, pp. 176−178 (= "Cinq élégies"); Milner−Storm 95 (= Molho, *Usos*); Molho, "Cinq élégies," no. 1 (p. 231); Molho, *Usos*, pp. 264−266, 330 (= "Cinq élégies"); PTJ 238 (= Molho, *Usos*); Sojo 4 (= Molho, *Usos*). See also Miguel Herrero, "El Pozo Airón," *Estudios Geográficos* (Madrid), 2 (1941), 567−573; Díaz Mas, *Poesía luctuosa*, pp. 166−167.
/CMP X13, L5.7−8; Vol. III, 35−37 (nos. 28A−28B).
////Argenti−Rose, II, 718−719; Ross, *Reisen*, p. 186; Baud-Bovy, *Textes*, pp. 284−288; NSR, p. 75, n. 65 (*Tò stoicheiōméno pēgádi* / *The Haunted Well*).

39. *La sierpe del río* (*í-o*) (*The River Snake*) (X15) (**Salonika**): Uncle and nephew go wandering through the fields. (They approach a palace or castle.) They are drinking wine and wagering as to which of them will kill (or subdue) the river snake (or the old woman of the river). One of them will use a sword; the other an iron knife. Further along the way (in Antequera), there is a mill that will not turn with water or wine, but which turns with the blood of little children (little orphans; little Christians).

The ballad of *La sierpe del río* ends our collection on an enigmatic note. With the texts currently at hand, the story remains essentially impenetrable. The uncle−nephew pair recall heroic figures of the medieval epic and the Carolingian *romances* (*Yoná*, pp. 91−92); yet here they can hardly be considered heroic, since they are in their cups and are intemperately wagering on each other's bravery. The river snake (or old woman of the river) suggests, perhaps, some connection with Greek folklore and folksong, where fluvial spirits (*stoicheià*) frequently occur (Samuel G. Armistead and Joseph H. Silverman, "A Judeo-Spanish Derivative of the Ballad of *The Bridge of Arta*," *JAF*, 76 [1963], 16−20; *Yoná*, pp. 361−362 and nn. 15−16; N. G. Politis, *Melétai perí toū bíou kaì tēs glóssēs toū hellēnikoū laoū: Parádoseis*, Vol. I [Athens: P. D. Sakellarios, 1904], 250 ff.). It is unclear whether the verses concerning the monstrous mill that grinds with children's blood (cf. *Yoná*, pp. 50−53) are merely *Wanderstrophen* or actually form part of this ballad and have some connection with the serpent or female ogre (?) of the river. Sometimes they appear before (Benardete) and sometimes after (Attias) the references to uncle and nephew and the snake (or old woman); elsewhere still (Díaz−Plaja) they are connected to another song (*La estrella diana* [CMP

AA40]). *La sierpe del río* is often associated with two other Salonikan ballads: *Mal me supo el vino* (CMP X16) and *Sufrir callando* (CMP L7). Vv. 10−15 of Benardete's version are a non-traditional elaboration based, perhaps, on some folktale.

   Bibliography: ASK 71(3); Attias 29.21−30; CMP X15; Díaz−Plaja 15.10−12.

THEMATIC CLASSIFICATION

A. Épicos—Ballads Based on the Spanish Epic

   A3. *Las quejas de Jimena (á-e)* (3) Jimena's Complaint: 1

   A9. *El destierro del Cid (á-o)* (5) The Banishment of the Cid: 1

B. Carolingios—Ballads Based on the French Epic

   B3. *Roncesvalles (í)* (20) The Battle of Roncevaux: 2

   B6. *El sueño de doña Alda (á-e)* (21) Lady Alda's Dream: 3

   B8. *Almerique de Narbona (í)* (20) Aymeri of Narbonne: 2

   B15. *Gaiferos jugador (á-e)* Gaiferos the Gambler: 4

   B17. *Melisenda insomne (á-e)* (28) Sleepless Melisenda: 3

   B20. *Rosaflorida y Montesinos (í-a)* (26) Rosaflorida and Montesinos: 5

C. Históricos—Historical Ballads

   C2. *Juan Lorenzo (á)* (12) Juan Lorenzo: 6, 29

   C12. *La muerte del duque de Gandía (í-a)* (14) The Death of the Duke of Gandía: 7

   C13. *La expulsión de los judíos de Portugal (í-o, í-a)* (13) The Exile of the Jews from Portugal: 8

   C14. *La muerte del príncipe don Juan (á-a)* (15) The Death of Prince John: 9

E. Bíblicos—Biblical Ballads

   E3. *El nacimiento y vocación de Abraham* (strophic) (30) The Birth and Vocation of Abraham: 10

   E5. *El sacrificio de Isaac (á-o)* (31) The Sacrifice of Isaac: 11

   E7. *El robo de Dina (ó)* (32) The Rape of Dinah: 12

   E17. *Tamar y Amnón (á-a)* (37) Thamar and Amnon: 13

F. Clásicos—Classical Antiquity

   F1. *Blancaflor y Filomena (é-a)* (100) Blancaflor and Filomena: 14

   F2. *Hero y Leandro (ó)* (41) Hero and Leander: 15

   F5. *El robo de Elena (á, á-o)* (43) The Abduction of Helen of Troy: 16

   F7. *Tarquino y Lucrecia (á-a)* (45) Tarquin and Lucrece: 17

   F8. *Virgilios (é)* (46) Virgil: 18

117

H. Cautivos y Presos—Prisoners and Captives

    H1. *Las hermanas reina y cautiva (í-a)* (48) The Two Sisters: Queen and Captive: 19

    H2. *Don Bueso y su hermana* (strophic) (49) Don Bueso and His Sister: 20

I. Vuelta del Marido—The Husband's Return

    I1. *La vuelta del marido (í)* (58) The Husband's Return: 21

    I2. *La vuelta del marido (é)* (59) The Husband's Return: 22

J. Amor Fiel—Faithful Love

    J1. *El conde Niño (á)* (55) The Persecuted Lovers: 23

    J5. *Diego León (á-a)* (63) Diego León: 24

K. Amor Desgraciado—Unhappy Love

    K2. *La amante abandonada* (polyas.) The Abandoned Mistress: 25

    K5. *El pájaro verde (á-a)* (66) The Green Bird: 26

L. Esposa Desgraciada—The Unfortunate Wife

    L1. *El conde Alarcos (í-a)* (64) Count Alarcos: 27

    L4. *La mala suegra (á-e)* (70) The Evil Mother-in-Law: 28

    L8. *La malcasada del pastor (ó)* (72) The Shepherd's Mismated Wife: 15, 29

    L13. *La mujer engañada (í-a)* (74) The Deceived Wife: 30

M. Adúltera—The Adulteress

    M14. *Las bodas en París (í)* (95) The Wedding Feast in Paris: 2

O. Raptos y Forzadores—Rape and Abduction

    O5. *El rapto (í-a)* (94) The Abduction: 31

    O7. *El forzador (í-a)* (96) The Abductor: 32

P. Incesto—Incest

    P1. *Silvana (í-a)* (98) Silvana: 33

    P2. *Delgadina (á-a)* (99) Delgadina: 34

Q. Mujeres Seductoras—Seductive Women

    Q1. *Gerineldo (í-o)* (101) Gerineldo: 35

S. Varias Aventuras Amorosas—Various Amorous Adventures

    S5. *Repulsa y compasión (á)* (115) Rejection and Compassion: 36

    S6. *El sueño de la hija* (polyas.) (68; 129) The Daughter's Dream: 37

X. Asuntos Varios—Various Subjects

    X13. *El pozo airón (ó)* The Bottomless Well: 38

    X15. *La sierpe del río (í-o)* The River Snake: 39

BIBLIOGRAPHY

A. Abbreviations of Journals, Serial Publications, and Organizations

AION = *Annali*: Istituto Universitario Orientale, Naples.

ALM = *Anuario de Letras*, Mexico City.

AmSeph = *The American Sephardi*, New York.

AnM = *Anuario Musical*, Barcelona.

AO = *Archivum*, Oviedo.

BAAEE = *Biblioteca de Autores Españoles*, Madrid.

BBMP = *Boletín de la Biblioteca Menéndez Pelayo*, Santander.

BHi = *Bulletin Hispanique*, Bordeaux.

BICC = *Thesaurus: Boletín del Instituto Caro y Cuervo*, Bogotá.

BN = *Blanco y Negro*, Madrid.

BRAE = *Boletín de la Real Academia Española*, Madrid.

BUG = *Boletín de la Universidad de Granada*, Granada.

CE = *Cultura Española*, Madrid.

C.S.I.C. = Consejo Superior de Investigaciones Científicas, Madrid.

C.S.M.P. = Cátedra-Seminario Menéndez Pidal.

CuH = *Cuadernos Hispanoamericanos*, Madrid.

Edoth = *Edoth*, Jerusalem.

ER = *Estudis Romànics*, Barcelona.

ESef = *Estudios Sefardíes*, Madrid.

EtB = *Études Balkaniques*, Sofia.

HR = *Hispanic Review*, Philadelphia.

JAF = *Journal of American Folklore*, Philadelphia.

JFI = *Journal of The Folklore Institute*, Bloomington.

JS = *Le Judaïsme Séphardi*, London.

JVF = *Jahrbuch für Volksliedforschung*, Berlin.

MPh = *Modern Philology*, Chicago.

NRFH = *Nueva Revista de Filología Hispánica*, Mexico City.

RABM = *Revista de Archivos, Bibliotecas y Museos*, Madrid.

RDTP = *Revista de Dialectología y Tradiciones Populares*, Madrid.

REJ = *Revue des Études Juives*, Paris.

Rĕšumôt = *Rĕšumôt*, Tel-Aviv.

RF = *Romanische Forschungen*, Köln.

RFE = *Revista de Filología Española*, Madrid.

RHi = *Revue Hispanique*, Paris.

RHM = *Revista Hispánica Moderna*, New York.

RPh = *Romance Philology*, Berkeley.

Sef = Sefarad, Madrid.
SFQ = Southern Folklore Quarterly, Gainesville, Florida.
Shevet va'Am = Shevet va'Am, Jerusalem.
SMe = Studi Medievali, Turin.
TI = Tribuna Israelita, Mexico City.
VR = Vox Romanica, Bern.
WF = Western Folklore, Berkeley-Los Angeles
Yedaᶜ–ᶜĀm = Yedaᶜ–ᶜĀm, Tel Aviv.
YIFMC = Yearbook of the International Folk Music Council, Kingston, Ontario.
ZRPh = Zeitschrift für Romanische Philologie, Tübingen.

B. Unedited Materials

Adatto MS =   Collection of 28 *romance* texts representing 19 different text-
                       types collected by Emma Adatto [Schlesinger], from Eastern
                       Sephardic informants, in Seattle, Washington, between 1931
                       and 1935. For other texts collected by E. Adatto, see CMP, III,
                       145–146, nos. 230–236.

Adatto Recordings =   Collection of 31 *romance* texts recorded on discs by Emma
                       Adatto [Schlesinger], from Eastern informants, in Seattle
                       (Washington), in 1935–1936.

Amiras MS =   Collection of numerous lyric couplets and six *romances* tran-
                       scribed by Max Mentesh Amiras (Salonika); photographic copy
                       acquired by Samuel G. Armistead and Joseph H. Silverman in
                       Los Angeles, August 8, 1958.

ASK =   Tape-recorded collection of Eastern and Moroccan Judeo-
                       Spanish *romances* formed by Samuel G. Armistead, Joseph H.
                       Silverman, and Israel J. Katz, between 1957 and 1980. The
                       collection comprises approximately 1,473 texts, fragments, and
                       major contaminations of *romances* and narrative songs (721
                       Eastern; 752 Moroccan) embodying some 186 text-types. The
                       major part of the collection was formed by S. G. A. and J. H. S.
                       with Eastern informants in the United States (1957–1960), by
                       I. J. K. in Israel (1959–1961), and by S. G. A., J. H. S., and
                       I. J. K. in Morocco (1962–1963); it also includes interviews by
                       S. G. A. in Los Angeles (1963), Philadelphia (1969), and Cam-
                       bridge, Mass. (1980), by S. G. A. and I. J. K. in New York
                       (1971), by I. J. K. in Israel (1971), and 205 texts and fragments
                       collected by S. G. A. and J. H. S. in Israel (1978). In the
                       present bibliography the total number of texts for a given theme
                       appears in parentheses following the text-type number.

Bendayán MS =   Notebook containing transcriptions of 8 Sephardic traditional poems, including four *romances* (representing 5 different text-types), belonging to Elías Bendayán (Tetuán); the *romance* texts were transcribed before 1936, some before August 7, 1924; photographic copy acquired by Samuel G. Armistead and Joseph H. Silverman, August, 1962.

Bennaim MS =   Manuscript collection of 91 texts of 80 different *romances* and narrative songs, formed in Tetuán by Luna Bennaim (1893–1958), between 1919 and 1950 (approximately). The MS was given to Iacob M. Hassán (C.S.I.C.) by Moisés Benolol.

Boas–Nahón =   Collection of 15 *romances* from Tangier sung by Suzanne Tole-dano and recorded on discs by Franz Boas and Zarita Nahón in New York between 1930 and 1936. See now Samuel G. Armistead, Israel J. Katz, and Joseph H. Silverman, "Judeo-Spanish Folk Poetry from Morocco (The Boas–Nahón Collection)," *YIFMC*, 11 (1979), 59–75.

Castro MS =   Collection of 59 *romances* transcribed by Américo Castro in Tetuán, Xauen, and Larache, during the winter of 1922. See Samuel G. Armistead and Joseph H. Silverman, "Un aspecto desatendido de la obra de Américo Castro," *Estudios sobre la obra de Américo Castro*, ed. Pedro Laín Entralgo and Andrés Amorós (Madrid: Taurus, 1971), pp. 181–190.

CMP =   Collection of 2,150 texts of *romances* and narrative songs, representing 298 different text-types, brought together by Ramón Menéndez Pidal, between 1896 and 1957 and housed at the Archivo Menéndez Pidal in Madrid. See CMP, in Published Sources.

Crews MS =   Collection of 37 *romances* and lyric songs collected in Salonika (1935) and Sarajevo (1929) by Cynthia M. Crews (26 texts from Salonika; 11 from Sarajevo), to be edited in *ESef*, 2 (in press). Samuel G. Armistead and Joseph H. Silverman, "Sobre los romances y canciones judeo-españoles recogidos por Cynthia M. Crews" will accompany the edition.

Essayag MS =   Collection of 8 *romance* texts, representing 9 different text-types, originally transcribed by Aarón D. Essayag (Tetuán); photographic copy acquired by Samuel G. Armistead, in Melilla, March 3, 1963.

Fereres MS =   Collection of 20 *romances* transcribed by Samuel Fereres in Larache (Morocco) before August 25, 1962, when the MS was acquired by Samuel G. Armistead, Joseph H. Silverman, and Israel J. Katz.

Librowicz (II) = Collection of 252 ballad texts representing 82 text-types from the Moroccan tradition (Tangier, Tetuán, Gibraltar) collected in Málaga, Marbella, Madrid, New York, Montreal, Caracas, and Migdal Ha-Emek (Israel), in 1971−1973. For the content of this collection, see Librowicz, *Florilegio*, pp. vii−ix, n. 2.

Luria MS = Collection of 18 *romances* and fragments collected by Max A. Luria in Monastir, Yugoslavia, in 1927, and now in possession of the Library of Yeshiva University, New York. Eight texts were published in Samuel G. Armistead and Joseph H. Silverman, ''Rare Judeo-Spanish Ballads from Monastir (Yugoslavia) Collected by Max A. Luria,'' *AmSeph*, 7−8 (1975), 51−61.

Milwitzky MS = Collection of 58 *romance* texts representing 26 text-types transcribed by William Milwitzky, in Eastern Mediterranean communities, in 1898 and 1899. See Samuel G. Armistead, Marius Sala, and Joseph H. Silverman, ''Un último eco del romancero sefardí de Bucarest,'' *ALM*, 10 (1972), 233−236; also *News of the Yivo*, no. 81 (January 1962), p. 3.

Onís = Collection of 22 Eastern Sephardic *romances* recorded on discs by Federico de Onís, in New York, in 1933, 1934, and 1935.

Pinto = Collection of 26 *romances* and traditional songs from Morocco tape-recorded by Abraham Pinto before 1978, when a copy of the tape was acquired by Joseph H. Silverman.

C. Published Sources

Abbot, George Frederick. *Songs of Modern Greece*. Cambridge: Cambridge University Press, 1900, ix + [2] + 307 pp.

Adatto = Adatto [Schlesinger], Emma. ''A Study of the Linguistic Characteristics of the Seattle Sefardi Folklore.'' M.A. thesis, University of Washington, 1935, iii + 116 pp.

AFC = Amades, Joan. *Folklore de Catalunya: Cançoner (Cançons— refranys—endevinalles)*. Barcelona: Selecta, 1951, 1,396 pp.

Algazi, Léon. *Chants séphardis*. London: Fédération Séphardite Mondiale, 1958, xvi + 63 pp.

―――. *Quatre mélodies judéo-espagnols pour chant et piano (ou harpe)*. Paris and New York: Editions Salabert, n. d.

Alonso−Blecua = Alonso, Dámaso, and J. M. Blecua. *Antología de la poesía española: Lírica de tipo tradicional*. 2d ed. Madrid: Gredos, 1969, lxxxvi + 265 pp.

Alvar, Manuel. "El romance de Gerineldo entre los sefarditas marroquíes," *BUG*, 23 (1951), 127—144.

———. "Cinco romances de asunto novelesco recogidos en Tetuán," *ER*, 3 (1951—1952), 57—87.

———. "Los romances de *La bella [en] misa* y de *Virgilios* en Marruecos," *AO*, 4 (1954), 264—276.

———. "Amnón y Tamar en el romancero marroquí," *VR*, 15 (1956), 241—258; reprinted in *El Romancero: Tradicionalidad*, pp. 225—241.

———. *Textos hispánicos dialectales: Antología histórica.* 2 vols. Madrid: *RFE*, Anejo LXXIII, 1960, xxvii + 919 pp.

———. *El Romancero: Tradicionalidad y pervivencia.* 2d ed. Barcelona: Planeta, 1974, 406 pp. + 23 maps.

———. *Cantos de boda judeo-españoles.* Madrid: C.S.I.C., 1971, xxv + 403 pp.

Arce, Agustín. "Cinco nuevos romances del Cid," *Sef*, 21 (1961), 69—75.

Argenti—Rose = Argenti, Philip P., and H. J. Rose. *The Folklore of Chios.* 2 vols. Cambridge: Cambridge University Press, 1949, xii + x + 1199 pp.

Armistead, Samuel G., and Joseph H. Silverman. "A New Collection of Judeo-Spanish Ballads," *JFI*, 3 (1966), 133—153.

———. "Arabic Refrains in a Judeo-Spanish *Romance*," *Iberoromania* (Munich), 2 (1970), 91—95.

———. "Un aspecto desatendido de la obra de Américo Castro," *Estudios sobre la obra de Américo Castro*, ed. Pedro Laín Entralgo and Andrés Amorós. Madrid: Taurus, 1971, pp. 181—190.

———. "El cancionero judeo-español de Marruecos en el siglo XVIII (*Incipits* de los Ben-Çûr)," *NRFH*, 22 (1973), 280—290.

———. "Romancero antiguo y moderno," *AION*, 16 (1974), 245—259.

———. "Siete vueltas dio al castillo," *RDTP*, 30 (1974), 323—326.

———. "Rare Judeo-Spanish Ballads from Monastir (Yugoslavia) Collected by Max A. Luria," *AmSeph*, 7—8 (1975), 51—61.

————. "Una variación antigua del romance de *Tarquino y Lucrecia*," *BICC*, 33 (1978), 122–126.

————. "Sobre los romances y canciones judeoespañoles recogidos por Cynthia M. Crews," *ESef*, 2 (in press).

Armistead, Samuel G., Marius Sala, and Joseph H. Silverman. "Un último eco del romancero sefardí de Bucarest," *ALM*, 10 (1972), 233–236.

ART =   Alonso Cortés, Narciso, "Romances tradicionales," *RHi*, 50 (1920), 198–268.

ASW =   Menéndez Pelayo, Marcelino. "Apéndices y suplemento a la *Primavera y flor de romances* de Wolf y Hoffmann," *Antología de poetas líricos castellanos*. IX, "Ed. Nac.," XXV. Santander: C.S.I.C., 1945, 467 pp.

Attias, Moshe, "Ha-rômansah šel Don Bu'ezo," *Edoth*, 1:4 (1946), 235–238.

————. "Ha-rômansah *Tarkînôs wĕ-Lûkreçîah* bi-kĕṭāb-yād šabĕṭa'î," *Shevet va'Am*, 3 (1959), 97–101.

Attias =   Attias, Moshe. *Romancero sefaradí: romanzas y cantes populares en judeo-español*. 2d ed. Jerusalem: Ben-Zewi Institute, 1961, 350 pp.

————. *Cancionero judeo-español: Canciones populares en judeo-español*. Jerusalem: Centro de Estudios sobre el Judaísmo de Salónica (Tel-Aviv), 1972, xi + 383 pp.

————. "Çĕrôr rômansôt bĕ-kt"y šel Sarayevo," *Shevet va'Am*, 2 (=7) (1973), 295–370.

Avenary, Hanoch. "Cantos españoles antiguos mencionados en la literatura hebrea," *AnM*, 25 (1971), 67–79.

Bar-Lewaw, Itzhak. "Aspectos del judeo-español de las comunidades sefardíes en Atlanta, Ga. y Montgomery, Ala. (EE.UU.)," *XI Congreso Internacional de Lingüística y Filología Románicas: Actas*. Ed. Antonio Quilis et al. IV, Madrid: *RFE*, Anejo LXXXVI, 1968, 2109–2124.

Baruch, Kalmi. "Španske romanse bosanskih Jevreja," *Godišnjak* (Sarajevo-Belgrade: "La Benevolencia" and "Potpora," 1933), pp. 272–288. Ed. and trans., "Spanish Ballads of the Bosnian Jews," *Bosnia*, pp. 31–58.

————. *Izabrana djela*. Sarajevo: Svjetlost, 1972, 415 pp.

Bassan [Warner], Susan. "Judeo-Spanish Folk Poetry." M.A. thesis, Columbia University, 1947, [4] + 165 pp.

Baud-Bovy, Samuel. *La Chanson populaire grecque du Dodé-canèse: Les Textes*. Paris: "Les Belles Lettres," 1936, 408 pp.

Benardete, Maír José. "Los romances judeo-españoles en Nueva York." M.A. thesis, Columbia University, 1923, xii +45 pp.

―――. "A Sheaf of Sephardic Songs," *JS*, 26 (1963), 1101 – 1110; also published in *La Voz* (New York), 8:7 (April 1963), 14 – 20.

Benarroch Pinto, Isaac. *El indiano, el kadi y la luna*. Tetuán: Editora Marroquí, 1951, 200 pp.

Bénichou =   Bénichou, Paul. *Romancero judeo-español de Marruecos*. Madrid: Castalia, 1968, 373 pp.

―――. *Creación poética en el romancero tradicional*. Madrid: Gredos, 1968, 190 pp.

Benmayor, Rina. "Oral Narrative and the Comparative Method: *The Judeo-Spanish Ballad Chapbooks of Yacob Abraham Yoná*," *RPh*, 31 (1977 – 1978), 501 – 521.

―――. *Romances judeo-españoles de Oriente: Nueva recolec-ción*. Madrid: C.S.M.P., 1979, 262 pp.

Benoliel, José. "Dialecto judeo-hispano-marroquí o hakitía," *BRAE*, 13 (1926), 209 – 233, 342 – 363, 507 – 538; 14 (1927), 137 – 168, 196 – 234, 357 – 373, 566 – 580; 15 (1928), 47 – 61, 188 – 223; 32 (1952), 255 – 289.

Besso, Henry V. "Los sefardíes y el idioma castellano," *RHM*, 34 (1968), 176 – 194.

Beutler, Gisela. *Estudios sobre el romancero español en Colom-bia en su tradición escrita y oral desde la época de la conquista hasta la actualidad*. Bogotá: Instituto Caro y Cuervo, 1977, xvi + 615 pp.

Bidjarano, Haim. "Los judíos españoles de Oriente: Lengua y literatura popular," *Boletín de la Institución Libre de Enseñanza* (Madrid), 9 (1885), 23 – 27.

Bosnia =   Armistead, Samuel G., and Joseph H. Silverman, with the collaboration of Biljana Šljivić-Šimšić. *Judeo-Spanish Ballads from Bosnia*. Philadelphia: University of Pennsylvania, 1971, x + 129 pp.

BR =

Yosef, Binyamin Bekar. *'El bukyeto de romansas*. Istanbul: Suhulet, 5686 (= 1926), 47 pp.; ed. of *romance* texts in Samuel G. Armistead and Joseph H. Silverman, with the collaboration of Iacob M. Hassán. *Seis romancerillos sefardíes*. Madrid: Castalia, 1981, chap. V (= SRC).

Braga =

Braga, Theóphilo. *Romanceiro geral português*. 2d ed., 3 vols. Lisbon: I–II, Manuel Gomes; III, J. A. Rodrigues, 1906–1909, viii + 639; 588; 633 pp.

Cantera Ortiz de Urbina, Jesús. *Los sefardíes*. 2d ed. (*Temas españoles*, no. 352). Madrid: Publicaciones Españolas, 1965, 31 pp.

Carré Alvarellos, Lois. *Romanceiro popular galego de tradizón oral*. Oporto: Junta Provincial do Douro Litoral, 1959, [vii] + 337 pp.

Catalán, Diego. *Por campos del Romancero: Estudios sobre la tradición oral moderna*. Madrid: Gredos, 1970, 309 pp.

———. "Memoria e invención en el Romancero de tradición oral," *RPh*, XXIV (1970–1971), 1–25, 441–463.

CBU =

Larrea Palacín, Arcadio de. "El cancionero de Baruh Uziel," *VR*, 18 (1959), 324–365.

Child =

Child, Francis James. *The English and Scottish Popular Ballads*. 5 vols. New York: Dover, 1965, xxxi + 508; ix + 515; ix + 521; ix + 525; ix + 569 + [55] pp.

CMP =

Armistead, Samuel G., with the collaboration of Selma Margaretten, Paloma Montero, and Ana Valenciano and with musical transcriptions edited by Israel J. Katz. *El romancero judeo-español en el Archivo Menéndez Pidal (Catálogo-índice de romances y canciones)*. 3 vols. Madrid: C.S.M.P., 1977, 387; 393; 358 pp.

Coello =

Menéndez Pelayo, Marcelino. "Romances castellanos tradicionales entre los judíos de Levante," *Antología de poetas líricos castellanos*, IX, "Ed. Nac.;" XXV, Santander: C.S.I.C., 1945, 387–439. We list separately nos. 1–4, 6, and 8–12, collected by Carlos Coello y Pacheco from the Salonikan tradition.

Cohen, Martine. *Recueil, édition et étude de textes enregistrés auprès de judéo-hispanophones originaires de Turquie et de Grèce à Paris en 1972*. Mémoire, Université de Paris IV: Institut d'Études Hispaniques, Paris, 1972–1973, 141 pp.

CVR =   Menéndez Pidal, Juan. *Poesía popular: Colección de los viejos romances que se cantan por los asturianos en la danza prima, esfoyazas y filandones*. Madrid: Hijos de J. A. García, 1885, xv + 360 pp.

Danon, Abraham. "Recueil de romances judéo-espagnoles chantées en Turquie," *REJ*, 32 (1896), 102–123, 263–275; 33 (1896), 122–139, 255–268.

DCELC =   Corominas, Joan. *Diccionario crítico etimológico de la lengua castellana*. 4 vols. Madrid: Gredos, 1954, lxviii + 995; [v] + 1081; [v] + 1117; 1224 pp.

Decombe, Lucien. *Chansons populaires recueillies dans le département d'Ille-et-Vilaine*. Rennes: H. Caillière, 1884, xxviii + 401 + 55 pp.

DgF =   Grundtvig, Svend, with Axel Olrik, Hakon Grüner-Nielsen, et al. *Danmarks gamle Folkeviser*. 12 vols. Copenhagen: Universitets-Jubilaeets Danske Samfund, 1966–1976, I: 10 + xvi + 428 + 47 pp.; II: 10 + xv + 682 pp.; III: 8 + xxv + 934 pp.; IV: 6 + [vi] + 903 pp.; V: 8 + [xi] + 390 + [ii] + 401 pp.; VI: 6 + [ix] + 474 pp.; VII: 6 + [vi] + 578 pp.; VIII–IX (in one vol.): 4 + [v] + 491 + [vi] + 241 pp.; X: [5] + xii + 910 pp.; XI: 126 + [ii] + 468 + [ii] + [xxiv] + 84 + [iv] + xxviii + 192 pp.; XII: 478 pp.

Díaz, Joaquín. *Palabras ocultas en la canción folklórica*. Madrid: Taurus, 1971, 143 pp.

Díaz Mas, María Paloma. *Poesía luctuosa judeo-española*. Memoria de Licenciatura, Universidad Complutense, Facultad de Filología, Madrid, 1977, [iii] + 262 pp.

Díaz-Plaja, Guillermo. "Aportación al cancionero judeo español del Mediterráneo oriental," *BBMP*, 16 (1934), 44–61.

Doncieux, George. *Le Romancéro populaire de la France: Choix de chansons populaires françaises*. Paris: Émile Bouillon, 1904, xliv + 522 pp.

DRH =   Armistead, Samuel G., and Joseph H. Silverman. *Diez romances hispánicos en un manuscrito sefardí de la Isla de Rodas*. Pisa: Istituto di Letteratura Spagnola e Ispano-Americana dell'Università di Pisa, 1962, 93 pp. (re-edited in TCR, Section A).

Durán, Agustín. *Romancero general o Colección de romances castellanos anteriores al siglo XVIII*. 2 vols. (*BAAEE* 10 and 16). Madrid: Atlas, 1945, xcvii + 600; xii + 736 pp.

DVM =   Meier, John, with Erich Seemann, Walter Wiora, H. Siuts, et al.
                 Deutsche Volkslieder mit ihren Melodien: Deutsche Volkslieder:
                 Balladen. 6 vols. I, Berlin and Leipzig: Walter de Gruyter,
                 1935; II, Berlin: Walter de Gruyter, 1939; III, 1954; IV, 1959;
                 V, Freiburg im Breisgau: Deutsches Volksliedarchiv, 1967; VI,
                 1976.

                 Elnecavé, David. "Folklore de los sefardíes de Turquía,"
                 reprinted from *Sef*, 23 (1963). References to *romances* allude to
                 the numbers in Section III.

                 Estrugo, José M. "Tradiciones españolas en las juderías del
                 Oriente Próximo (Reminiscencias y apuntes)," *Sef*, 14 (1954),
                 128–147.

                 ———. *Los sefardíes.* Havana: Lex, 1958, 146 pp.

                 ———. "Reminiscencias de la judería sefardí del cercano
                 Oriente," *RDTP*, 14 (1958), 70–77.

ETA =   Armistead, Samuel G., and Joseph H. Silverman. "The Judeo-
                 Spanish Ballad Chapbook *'Endeğas de Ɵišᶜāh bĕ-'Āb*," *HR*,
                 38:5 (1970), 47–55 (reprinted in SRC, Chap. IV).

                 Fernández, Africano. *España en Africa y el peligro judío:*
                 Apuntes de un testigo desde 1915 a 1918. Santiago de Com-
                 postela: El Eco Franciscano, 1918, 328 pp.

FM =   Catalán, Diego, with the collaboration of María Jesús López de
                 Vergara, Mercedes Morales, Araceli González, María Victoria
                 Izquierdo, and Ana Valenciano. *La flor de la marañuela:*
                 Romancero general de las Islas Canarias. 2 vols. Madrid:
                 C.S.M.P., 1969, ix + 367; vii + 266 pp.

                 Frenk Alatorre, Margit. "El Cancionero sevillano de la Hispanic
                 Society (ca. 1568)," *NRFH*, 16 (1962), 355–394.

FRS =   Armistead, Samuel G., and Joseph H. Silverman. *Flor de*
                 romances sefardíes. (In preparation)

                 Frye, Ellen. *The Marble Threshing Floor: A Collection of Greek*
                 Folksongs. Austin and London: University of Texas Press for
                 The American Folklore Society, 1973, xvi + 327 pp.

Galante =   Galante, Abraham. "Quatorze romances judéo-espagnols,"
                 RHi, 10 (1903), 594–606.

Gallent =   Guastavino Gallent, Guillermo. "Cinco romances sefardíes,"
                 Africa (Madrid), 8:119 (November 1951), 537–539.

García Figueras, Tomás. "*El sacrificio de Isaac* (Romance de asunto bíblico)," *Homenaje a Millás-Vallicrosa*. Vol. I. Barcelona: C.S.I.C., 1954, 697−700.

Gerson-Kiwi, Edith. "El legado de la música judía a través de los tiempos," *Bitfutzot Hagolá: Estudios y reseñas sobre el movimiento sionista y el mundo judío*. Jerusalem: Organización Sionista Mundial, Sección de Estudios de la Diáspora, 1964, pp. 146−169; also published as "The Legacy of Jewish Music Through the Ages," *In the Dispersion: Surveys and Monographs on the Jewish World*. III. Jerusalem: World Zionist Organization, Organization Department, Research Section, 1963−1964, pp. 149−172.

Gil =   Gil, Rodolfo. *Romancero judeo-español*. Madrid: Imprenta Alemana, 1911, cxxiv + 140 pp.

Giménez Caballero, Ernesto. "Monograma sobre la judería de Escopia," *ROcc*, 8:81 (1930), 356−376.

González-Llubera, Ignacio. "Three Jewish Spanish Ballads in MS. *British Museum Add*. 26967," *MAe*, 7 (1938), 15−28.

Granell Muñiz, Manuel. "Fragmento del diario," *Juventud en el mundo antiguo (Crucero universitario por el Mediterráneo)*. Ed. Carlos A. Del Real, Julián Marías, and Manuel Granell. Madrid: Espasa-Calpe, 1934, pp. 255−305.

Haboucha, Reginetta. "Judeo-Spanish Ballads from Israel," *El Romancero hoy: Nuevas fronteras (2° Coloquio Internacional, University of California, Davis)*. Ed. Antonio Sánchez Romeralo, Diego Catalán, and Samuel G. Armistead. Madrid: C.S.M.P. and University of California, 1979, pp. 105−112.

HBS =   Armistead, Samuel G., and Joseph H. Silverman. "Hispanic Balladry among the Sephardic Jews of the West Coast," *WF*, 19 (1960), 229−244.

Hemsi, Alberto. *Coplas sefardíes (Chansons judéo-espagnoles) [pour chant et piano]*. 10 fascicles, I−V. Alexandria: Édition Orientale de Musique, 1932−1938, VI−X. Aubervilliers: privately printed, 1969−1973, I: xiii + 16; II: xii + 29; III: xviii + 29; IV: xviii + 35; V: xxii + 29; VI: xiv + 29; VII: xii + 26; VIII: viii + 28; IX: vi + 32; X: xxvii + 40 pp.

———. "Sur le folklore séfardi," *JS*, 18 (April 1959), 794−795.

———. "Évocation de la France dans le folklore séphardi," *JS*,

24 (July 1962), 1055–1057, 1059; 25 (December 1962), 1091–1093.

Hollander, Mónica E. "Reliquias del romancero judeo-español de Oriente." Ph.D. dissertation, University of Pennsylvania, 1978, ix + 297 pp.

Jungić, B. "Tri sefardske romanse," *Godišnjak*. Sarajevo and Belgrade: "La Benevolencia" and "Potpora," 1933, pp. 289–292 (reprinted in *Bosnia*, pp. 59–62).

Kaludova, Stamatka. "Sur la poésie et la musique des juifs de la Péninsule Balkanique, du XVe au XXe siècle," *EtB*, 6:2 (1970), 98–123.

Katz, Israel J. "Toward a Musical Study of the Judeo-Spanish *Romancero*," *WF*, 21 (1962), 83–91.

———. "Ladino Literature: The Musical Tradition of the *Romancero*." *Encyclopaedia Judaica*, X. Jerusalem and New York: Macmillan, 1971, cols. 1351–1353.

———. *Judeo-Spanish Traditional Ballads from Jerusalem: An Ethnomusicological Study*. 2 vols. New York: Institute of Mediaeval Music, 1972–1975, ix + 203 pp.; [ii] + 47 + iii-xix pp.

Kayserling, Meyer. *Biblioteca española-portugueza-judaica: Dictionnaire bibliographique*. Nieuwkoop: B. De Graaf, 1961, xxi + 155 pp.

Larrea =   Larrea Palacín, Arcadio de. *Romances de Tetuán*, 2 vols. Madrid: C.S.I.C., 1952, 351; 377 pp.

Larrea Palacín, Arcadio de. "Romances hispánicos del Medioevo," *Mundo Hispánico* (Madrid), 5:49 (April 1952), 51–54.

Lazar, Moshe. *The Sephardic Tradition: Ladino and Spanish-Jewish Literature*. New York: W. W. Norton, 1972, 222 pp.

Levy =   Levy, Isaac. *Chants judéo-espagnols*. 4 vols. I, London: Fédération Séphardite Mondiale [1959], II, Jerusalem: Édition de l'auteur, 1970; III, Jerusalem: Édition de l'auteur, 1971; IV, Jerusalem: Édition de l'auteur, 1973, viii + 87; [viii] + 104; [vii] + 121; [vii] + 124 pp.

Levy, Isaac. *Antología de liturgia judeo-española*. 9 vols. Jerusalem: División de Cultura del Ministerio de Educación y Cultura, I (1964), xxx + 176; II (n.d.), xix + 272; III (n.d.), xxiv + 512; IV (n.d.), xxiii + 520; V (1973), xxiv + 421; VI (1974), xv + 419; VII (1975), xii + [1] + 196; VIII (1976), xiv + [1] + 267; IX (1977), xvi + [1] + 434 pp.

Librowicz = Librowicz, Oro Anahory. "Florilegio de romances sefardíes de la diáspora. Ph.D. Dissertation, Columbia University, New York, 1974, xi + 201 pp.

————. "Romances judeo-españoles de Gibralter," *ESef* (in press).

Lida, Denah Levy. "El sefardí esmirniano de Nueva York." Ph.D. dissertation, Universidad Nacional Autónoma de México, 1952, 152 pp.

LSO = Molho, Michael. *Literatura sefardita de Oriente*. Madrid and Barcelona: C.S.I.C., 1960, xxvii + 426 pp.

MacCurdy, Raymond, and Daniel D. Stanley. "Judeo-Spanish Ballads from Atlanta, Georgia," *SFQ*, 15 (1951), 221–238.

Mano = Levis Mano, Guy, ed. and trans. *Romancero judéo-espagnol*. Paris: GLM, 1971, 93 pp.

Manrique de Lara, Manuel. "Romances españoles en los Balkanes," *BN*, 26:1285 (January 2, 1916), 3 pages (no pagination).

————. "Leonor Telles en el romancero judaico-español," *Correo Erudito* (Madrid), 2:8 ([1940?]), 299.

Mendoza, Vicente T. *El romance español y el corrido mexicano: Estudio comparativo*. Mexico City: Universidad Nacional Autónoma, 1939, xviii + 835 pp.

Menéndez Pidal, Ramón. "El Romancero y los sefardíes," *TI*, 5:51 (February 1949), pp. xxi–xxii.

————. "El romancero sefardí: Su extraordinario carácter conservador," *The Sephardi Heritage: Essays on the History and Cultural Contribution of the Jews of Spain and Portugal*. Ed. Richard D. Barnett. Vol. I. New York: Ktav, 1971, 552-559.

Mézan, Saúl. Hā-'Agādôt ha-měšîhiyôt ba-šîrāh hā-ᶜāmāmît hā-'išpanyôlît," *Mizrāḥ û-Maᶜărāb* (Jerusalem), 2 (1929), 205–213.

Milá = Milá y Fontanals, Manuel. *Romancerillo catalán: Canciones tradicionales*. 2d ed. Barcelona: Alvaro Verdaguer, 1882, xix + 459 pp.

Milner—Storm =   Milner, Chanah, and Paul Storm. *Sefardische liederen en balla-den: Romanzas*. The Hague: Albersen, 1974, 115 pp.

Milwitzky, William. "El viajero filólogo y la antigua España," *Cuba y América* (Havana), 19:17 (July 23, 1905), 307–309, 325–327.

Molho, Michael. "Cinq élégies en judéo-espagnol," *BHi*, 42 (1940), 231–235.

———. *Usos y costumbres de los sefardíes de Salónica*. Madrid and Barcelona: C.S.I.C., 1950, 341 pp.

———. "Tres romances de tema bíblico y dos canciones de cuna," *Comentario* (Buenos Aires), 4:15 (April–June, 1957), 64–70.

Moya, Ismael. "Romances judeo-españoles en Buenos Aires." In *Romancero: Estudios sobre materiales de la colección de folklore*. 2 vols. Buenos Aires: Universidad, 1941. II, 255–259.

MP =   Menéndez Pidal, Ramón. "Catálogo del romancero judío-español," *CE*, 4 (1906), 1045–1077; 5 (1907), 161–199.

MPelayo =   Menéndez Pelayo, Marcelino. "Romances castellanos tradicionales entre los judíos de Levante," *Antología de poetas líricos castellanos*, IX, "Ed. Nac.," XXV, Santander: C.S.I.C., 1945, 387–439 (exclusive of those texts collected by Carlos Coello y Pacheco).

MRuiz =   Martínez Ruiz, Juan. "Poesía sefardí de carácter tradicional (Alcazarquivir)," *AO*, 13 (1963), 79–215.

Nahón =   Armistead, Samuel G., and Joseph H. Silverman, with the collaboration of Oro Anahory Librowicz. *Romances judeo-españoles de Tánger (recogidos por Zarita Nahón)*. Madrid: C.S.M.P., 1977, 255 pp.

Nigra, Costantino. *Canti popolari del Piemonte*. Turin: Giulio Einaudi, 1957, lxxiv + 765 pp.

[Noga] Alberti, Eleonora A. "Romances tradicionales en Latinoamérica: Algunos ejemplos sefaradíes y criollos," *Comunidades judías de Latinoamérica (1973–1975)*. Buenos Aires: Federación Sefaradí Latinoamericana, 1973–1975, pp. 252–269.

NSR =   Armistead, Samuel G., and Joseph H. Silverman. "A New Sephardic *Romancero* from Salonika," *RPh*, 16 (1962–1963), 59–82.

Ontañón de Lope, Paciencia. "Veintisiete romances del siglo XVI," *NRFH*, 15 (1961), 180–192.

Ortega, Manuel L. *Los hebreos en Marruecos*. 3d ed. Madrid: Compañía Ibero-Americana de Publicaciones, 1929, ix + 371 pp.

Primav. =   Wolf, Fernando J., and Conrado Hofmann. *Primavera y flor de romances*. 2 vols. Berlin: A. Ascher, 1856, xci + 357; [ii] + 432 pp. 2d ed., Marcelino Menéndez Pelayo. *Antología de poetas líricos castellanos*, VIII, "Ed. Nac.," XXIV, Santander: C.S.I.C., 1945, ix + 467 pp.

PTJ =   Alvar, Manuel. *Poesía tradicional de los judíos españoles*. Mexico City: Porrúa, 1966, lx + 295 pp.

Pulido =   Pulido Fernández, Ángel. *Intereses nacionales: Españoles sin patria y la raza sefardí*. Madrid: E. Teodoro, 1905, viii + 663 pp.

Rechnitz, Florette M. "Tres romances de Tánger," and Israel J. Katz "On the Music of the Three *Romances* from Tangier," *ESef*, 1 (1978), 120–131.

RLH =   Menéndez Pidal, Ramón, and María Goyri de Menéndez Pidal. *Romancero tradicional de las lenguas hispánicas (Español— portugués—catalán—sefardí)*. Ed. Diego Catalán et al. 11 vols., Madrid: C.S.M.P., I: 1957, viii + 277 pp.; II: 1963, vii + 299 pp.; III: 1969, 207 pp.; IV: 1970, 285 pp.; V: 1971– 1972, 305 pp.; VI: 1975, 254 pp.; VII: 1975, 266 pp.; VIII, 1976, 454 pp.; IX, ed. Antonio Sánchez Romeralo and Ana Valenciano, 1977, 403 pp.; X: 1977–1978, 258 pp.; XI: 1977–1978, 223 pp.

Rodrigo, Joaquín. "Dos canciones sefardíes armonizadas," *Sef*, 14 (1954), 353–362.

Rodríguez-Moñino, Antonio. *Cancionero de romances (Anvers, 1550)*. Madrid: Castalia, 1967, 333 pp.

RoH =   Menéndez Pidal, Ramón. *Romancero hispánico (hispano-portugués, americano y sefardí)*. 2 vols. Madrid: Espasa-Calpe, 1953, xx + 407; 474 pp.

Rolland, Eugène. *Recueil de chansons populaires*. 6 vols. in 3. Paris: G.-P. Maisonneuve et Larose, 1967, [v] + 347; [ii] + 275; [ii] + 75 + [iv] + 75 + [iv] + 75 + [iv] + 83 pp.

Romano, Menahem. "Romances judéo-espagnoles," *JS*, No. 73 (January 1957), p. 601.

Romey, David. "A Study of Spanish Tradition in Isolation as Found in the Romances, Refranes, and Storied Folklore of the Seattle Sephardic Community." M.A. thesis, University of Washington, 1950, iv + 118 + xi pp.

Ross, Ludwig. *Reisen auf den griechischen Inseln des ägäischen Meeres*. III. Stuttgart-Tübingen: J. G. Cotta'scher Verlag, 1845, xvi + 192 pp.

RPC =   Alonso Cortés, Narciso. *Romances populares de Castilla*. Valladolid: Eduardo Sáenz, 1906, 128 pp.

RPM =   Cossío, José María de, and Tomás Maza Solano. *Romancero popular de La Montaña: Colección de romances tradicionales*. 2 vols. Santander: Sociedad Menéndez y Pelayo, 1933–1934, 479; 451 pp.

RQDB-I =   Goyri de Menéndez Pidal, María. "Romances que deben buscarse en la tradición oral," *RABM*, 10 (1906), 374–386; 11 (1907), 24–36; offprint: Madrid: *RABM*, 1907, 30 pp.

RTCN =   *Romances tradicionales y canciones narrativas existentes en el Folklore español* (*Incipit y temas*). Barcelona: Instituto Español de Musicología, 1945, 71 pp.

RVP =   Michaëlis de Vasconcelos, Carolina. *Estudos sôbre o Romanceiro peninsular: Romances velhos em Portugal*. 2d ed. Coimbra: Universidade, 1934, xi + 320 pp.

Sánchez Moguel, Antonio. "Un romance español en el dialecto de los judíos de Oriente," *BRAE*, 16 (1890), 497–509.

———. "Dos romances del Cid conservados en las juderías de Marruecos," *RF*, 23 (1907), 1087–1091.

San   S[an] S[ebastián], P. José Antonio de. *Canciones sefardíes para
Sebastián =   canto y piano*, Tolosa, Spain: Laborde y Labayen [ca. 1945], 19 pp.

Salavin, Pierre. *Les Séphardims d'Izmir et la tradition littéraire orale*. Mémoire de Maîtrise, Université de Grenoble, 1967–1968 [no pagination].

SBS =   Levy, Isaac Jack. "Sephardic Ballads and Songs in the United States: New Variants and Additions." M.A. thesis, University of Iowa, 1959, 297 pp.

Sciaky, Leon. *Farewell to Salonica: Portrait of an Era*. New York: A. A. Wyn, 1946, ix + 241 pp.

SICh =   Armistead, Samuel G., and Joseph H. Silverman. "Judeo-Spanish Ballads in a Ms by Salomon Israel Cherezli," *Studies in Honor of M. J. Benardete: Essays in Hispanic and Sephardic Culture*. Ed. Izaak A. Langnas and Barton Sholod. New York: Las Américas, 1965, pp. 367–387 (re-edited in *TCR*, section B).

Simoni, Wolf. *4 cànticas sefardìes: Chants populaires*. Paris: La Sirène Musicale [ca. 1937], 12 pp.

Sojo, V[icente] E[milio]. *Nueve canciones de los sefardíes de Salónica*. Cáracas: Dirección de la Escuela de Música "José Ángel Lamas," 1964, 13 pp.

Spomenica =   Kamhi, Samuel, ed. *Spomenica: 400 godina od dolaska jevreja u Bosnu i Hercegovinu (1566–1966)*. Sarajevo: "Oslobođenje," 1966, 368 pp.

SR =   Yosef, Binyamin Bekar. *Sēfer rēnānôt*. Jerusalem; no publisher, 5668 (= 1908), xxxii + 16 pp. Ed. of *romance* texts in Samuel G. Armistead and Joseph H. Silverman, with the collaboration of Iacob M. Hassán, *Seis romancerillos sefardíes*. Madrid: Castalia, 1981, Chap. V (= SRC).

SRC =   Armistead, Samuel G., and Joseph H. Silverman, with the collaboration of Iacob M. Hassán. *Seis romancerillos de cordel sefardíes*. Madrid: Castalia, 1981.

Tarica, Ralph. "Sephardic Culture in Atlanta," *South Atlantic Bulletin* (S.A.M.L.A., Chapel Hill, N.C.), 25:4 (March 1960), 1–5.

TCR =   Armistead, Samuel G., and Joseph H. Silverman. *Tres calas en el romancero sefardí (Rodas, Jerusalén, Estados Unidos)*. Madrid: Castalia, 1979, 198 pp.

Thomas, Romain. "Huit romances judéo-espagnols," *Hommage à Ernest Martinenche: Études hispaniques et américaines*. Paris: Editions d'Artrey (ca. 1940), pp. 282–292.

Torner, Eduardo M. *Temas folklóricos: Música y poesía*. Madrid: Faustino Fuentes, 1935, 155 pp.

————. *Lírica hispánica: Relaciones entre lo popular y lo culto*. Madrid: Castalia, 1966, 461 pp.

UR =   Uziel, Baruch. "Ha-folklor šel ha-yēhûdîm ha-sēfārādîm," *Rēšumô<u>t</u>*, 5 (1927), 324–337; 6 (1930), 359–397.

UYA =   Uziel, Baruch, "Šālōš rômansô<u>t</u>: Mi-pî yēhûdîm sēfārādîm," pp. 75–76; "Šālôš rômansôt: Mi-pî yĕhûdê Sĕfārad," pp. 172–177; "Šĕtê rômansôt: Min ha-folklor ha-yĕhûdî ha-sĕfārādî," pp. 261-265, *Yedaʿ-ʿĀm*, 2 (1953–1954).

Valls, Manuel. *Canciones sefarditas para soprano, flauta, y guitarra*. Madrid: Unión Musical Española, 1975, 16 pp.

VRP =   Leite de Vasconcellos, José. *Romanceiro português*. 2 vols. Coimbra: Universidade, 1958–1960, xxxiii + 481; [v] + 555 pp.

Wiener, Leo. "Songs of the Spanish Jews in the Balkan Peninsula," *MPh*, 1 (1903–1904), 205–216, 259–274.

Yoná =   Armistead, Samuel G., and Joseph H. Silverman. *The Judeo-Spanish Ballad Chapbooks of Yacob Abraham Yoná*. Berkeley, Los Angeles, and London: University of California Press, 1971, xlii + 640 pp.

Yurchenco, Henrietta. "Taping History in Morocco," *The American Record Guide* (New York), 24:4 (December, 1957), 130–132, 175.

INDEXES

Index of Geographic Origins

Index of Ballad Titles

Index of First Verses

GLOSSARY

The glossary lists only Arabic, Hebrew, and Turkish loan words and dialect forms which might offer some difficulty to understanding the texts and are not easily located in standard sources concerning Judeo-Spanish dialectology. Turkish references follow the *New Redhouse Turkish—English Dictionary* (Istanbul: Redhouse Yayınevi, 1968); Moroccan Arabic references are according to Henry Mercier, *Dictionnaire arabe—français* (Rabat: Les Editions "La Porte," 1951).

abultar 'to abort' 23*B*.4*b*.
afearéx: *See* **afiar**.
afiar 'give credit to'; *afearéx* 25.8*b*.
algüenga 'tongue' 14.13*b*.
aljadrar 'to appear'; *aljadra* 5.8*a*; *aljadró* 11.18*a* (read *alhadrar*, etc.) (M. Ar. *hader* 'présent, spectateur, assistant').
an: *See* **en**.
anxugare 'trousseau' 3.19*b*, 21*b*.
arexclat 'a type of cloth' 29.14*b* (origin?).
asarrear 'to cling; to wrap around' 23*A*.28*b* (T. *sarmak*).
asufare 'pearl trimming' 5.11*b* (read *ažufare*) (Sp. *aljófar*; with the *al-* "re-Arabized" perhaps under the influence of M. Ar. *juhar* 'perle; pierres précieuses' and other Ar. def. arts. assimilated to "sun letters"; accentuation would normally be *ažófar*).
asumar: *sin asumar* 'incalculable in number' 6.6*b*.
azojar 'orange, lemon, citron blossom' 22.21*b* (Sp. *azahar*; perhaps influenced by M. Ar. *zher* 'fleur d'oranger').
babé: meaning? 22.5*b*. See Bénichou, pp. 227–228.
bacxíx 'tip, reward, gift' 7*B*.12*b* (T. *bahşiş*).
baklavalí 'for making sweet pastry' (T. *baklava* + *li*).
baque 'sound (of a blow)' 7*C*.5*a* (cf. Port. *baque* 'thud, thump, crash').
barabar 'together' 14.10*b*. (T. *beraber*; Dialectal T. *barabar*).

calpáx 'cape' (?) 7C.11a (T. *kalpak* 'fur cape' + *tarpoş* 'skull cap, fez' + Sp. *capa* (?)).

cara haberes 'bad news' 28B.24a (T. *kara* 'black' + *haber* 'news').

cara sazán 'black carp' 23A.22b (T. *kara sazán*).

caronale 'related by blood' 4.6b; 'beloved' 3.8b, 18b.

carta 'paper' 34.1b. See CMP, III, 342, s.v.

cavesal 'neck (of a shirt)' 7B.8a; *cavesale* 3.22b.

comlesa 'mistress of a married man' 34.8a (Cast. *combleza*).

conchá: *See* **conjá**.

conjá 'rose' 23A.16b; *conchá* 12.1b (read *conjá*) (T. *konca* '[flower] bud').

contentés 'happiness, satisfaction' 28B.9b.

corbán 'sacrifice' 11.3b, 11b (H. *kārbān*).

covado 'coward' 4.10a.

crueldade 'cruelty' 4.17b (read *fieldade* 'faith, fidelity'). See *Yoná*, p. 636, s.v.

cuertas: *See* **güertas**.

descabeñada 'dishevelled' 9A.10b, 11b.

dulque 'duke' 7B.7a; *dunque* 7C.8a.

dunque: *See* **dulque**.

elflé: meaning? 22.4b (usually *un aciprés* 'cypress tree').

emburujar 'to wrap in, to envelop in': *emburujó* 2.15a.

en (read *an*) = Sp. personal *a* (as used before a vowel) 32.6b.

encapiado 'covered with hoods or cowls (?)' 11.25b (Sp. *capilla*).

enfalta: *See* **infalta**.

ente meaning? 20B.16. Asturian has *ente* 'entre', but we have not found the form in J.-Sp. See *DCELC*, II, s.v. *entre*. Aragonese and Morisco *enta* 'hacia' (probably from Ar. *'inda* 'at, near') is not satisfactory either. See Manuel Alvar, *El dialecto aragonés* (Madrid: Gredos, 1953), pp. 250–251, 317–318; Alvaro Galimés de Fuentes, *El libro de las batallas*, 2 vols. (Madrid: Gredos, 1975), II, 191; Reinhold Kontzi, *Aljamiado Texte*, 2 vols. (Wiesbaden: Steiner, 1974), I, 261.

envicitada: meaning (?) 9A.4b (usually *enveyutada* 'woolly').

extunico 'some article of clothing (?)' 30.13b.

favor 'fear' 12.4a.

galza 'heron' 3.17b, 18a.

gancho 'hook' 7A.6a; *gango* 7B.6a; *ganchera* 7A.6a; *gangero* 7B.6a; *gancho* 'anchor' 16.13b.

ganchera: *See* **gancho**.

gangero: *See* **gancho**.

gango: *See* **gancho**.

gansas 31.1b. See commentary.

garbe 'bearing, stance' 2.19a.

gravina: *See* **graviyina**.

graviyina 'pink (flower)' 23A.16a; *gravina* 32.1b.

güertas 'doors' 23B.5a (read *cuertas*). See Benoliel, *BRAE*, 13 (1926), 227.

guimará 'prayer book' 10.15b (H. *gĕmārā'*, *gĕmārāh* literally 'completion; tradition';

the term designates the *Talmud* or, more specifically, the second and supplementary part of the *Talmud*, providing a commentary on the first part, i.e., the *Mishnah*).

haberjí 'messenger' 8.6*b* (T. *haberci*).

hayá 'animal' 10.18*b* (H. *hayāh*).

imperalde 'emperor' 3.1*a*, 7*b*.

infalta 'princess' 27.5*a*; *enfalta* 27.1*a*.

jinjeví 'ginger' 21.8*b*.

meará 'cave' 10.8*a*, 14*b* (H. *mĕʿārāh*).

meatad 'middle' 13.18*a*, 29.19*a*, 36.3*a*.

mantil 'cloth' 2.15*a* (Sp. *mantel* 'table cloth' + T. *mendil* 'handkerchief, napkin, towel'; however J.-Sp. *mantil* could also be purely Hispanic in origin; cf. Cast. *mandil* 'apron; cleaning rag'; Valencian *mantil*; see *DCELC*, s.v. *mantel*).

mejatré 'accuser' 11.18*a*, 22*a* (H. *mĕkatrēg*). See Iacob M. Hassán, "Más hebraísmos en la poesía sefardí de Marruecos: Realidad y ficción léxicas," *Sef*, 37 (1977), 373–428: p. 405.

mezeliques 'appetizers' 15.14*a* (T. *mezelik*).

milsa 'chapel' 4.11*a*.

pechita 'napkin' 30.10*b* (T. *peçete*).

perquia 'perch' 23A.22*a* (Cast. *perca* + Gk. *pérkē*?).

pexquek: *See* **pexquéx**.

pexquéx 'gift, reward' 7C.13*b*; *pexquek* 7A.12*b* (T. *peşkeş* 'gift or offering brought to a superior').

rizá 'scarf' 9A.6*b* (T. *rida* 'woolen cloak; scarf for the shoulders').

ronjar 'to throw'; *ronjó* 24.31*b*; *ronjara* 13.16*b*.

ruxibón 'nightingale' 23.3*b*.

sacsís 'flower pots' 32.1*b* (T. *saksı*).

sanjí = *San Gil* 2.3*b*.

saray 'palace' 28B.2*b* (T. *saray*).

simán 'sign' 28B.17*a*, 18*a*, 26*a* (H. *simān*).

sirma 'silver thread' 3.5*a*, 20*b*, 22*b*, 7C.9*b* (T. *sırma*).

umá 'as for' 11.2*a*, 24*a*, 13.20*a* (M. Ar. *wa-amma*, *wamma* 'quant à').

virgüela 'guitar' 6.4*a*, 33.2*a*.

viz'ero 'missal' 35.41*b* (Sp. **mizero* < *misal*, with possible influence from *librito* [*de*] *rezar*?). See Nahón, pp. 67–68, nn. 7–8.

yelado 'cold, frozen' 20A.25*b*.

yinda 'just, even, only' 2.20*b*.

zihud 'merit' 10.22*a* (H. *zĕkût* 'merit; privilege; right; credit').